Carousel Parkway
and other poems

Books by AARON KRAMER

Poetry

Another Fountain
Till the Grass Is Ripe for Dancing
Thru Our Guns
The Glass Mountain
The Thunder of the Grass
The Golden Trumpet
Thru Every Window!
Denmark Vesey
Roll the Forbidden Drums!
The Tune of the Calliope
Moses
Rumshinsky's Hat
Henry at the Grating
On the Way to Palermo
O Golden Land!

Translation

The Poetry and Prose of Heinrich Heine
Morris Rosenfeld: The Teardrop Millionaire
Goethe, Schiller, Heine: Songs and Ballads
Rilke: Visions of Christ

Criticism

The Prophetic Tradition in American Poetry: 1835–1900
Melville's Poetry: Toward the Enlarged Heart

Contributions to Symposia

Seven Poets in Search of an Answer
Poetry Therapy
Poetry the Healer

Anthology

On Freedom's Side

Carousel Parkway
and other poems

Aaron Kramer

selected and with an introduction by Charles Fishman

*This edition is limited to
six hundred numbered copies,
of which this is
Number* 210

SAN DIEGO • NEW YORK
A. S. BARNES & COMPANY, INC.
IN LONDON:
THE TANTIVY PRESS

Carousel Parkway Poems text copyright © 1980 by Aaron Kramer

A. S. Barnes and Co., Inc.

The Tantivy Press
Magdalen House
136-148 Tooley Street
London SE1 2TT, England

First Edition
Manufactured in the United States of America
For information write to A. S. Barnes and Company, Inc.,
P.O. Box 3051, San Diego, CA 92038

Library of Congress Cataloging in Publication Data

Kramer, Aaron, 1921-
   Carousel Parkway, and other poems.

   I. Title.
PS3521.R29A17   1980   811'.5'4   78-75314
ISBN: 0-498-2386-9

1 2 3 4 5 6 7 8 9 84 83 82 81 80

Contents

Acknowledgments

To *The Antigonish Review* (Canada), for "Last Night in Brussels"; *Arion's Dolphin*, for "Ghosts"; *Carleton Miscellany*, for "Bay Parkway," "Forebodings," "Now, Before Shaving," and "Softening"; *English Journal*, for "Nocturne"; *Epos* (anthology), for "In the Geneve Lobby"; *Freedomways*, for "Attica in the Suburbs"; *Icarus*, for "Granddaughter on Beach"; *Islip Arts Review*, for "Location" and "Rain"; *Journal of Humanistic Psychology*, for "Thanksgiving Day" and "Visiting Hour"; *Mediterranean Review*, for "Piazza del Campidoglio"; *Midstream*, for "Coney Island" and "Zudioska"; *Modern Poetry Studies*, for "Carousel Parkway," "Glasses," "Kennedy Airport," "The Last Supper," "The Month Is Ripening," "Mr. Glicklich Takes a Shower," "Quebec," "Sunset," and "Two Visits"; *Orbis* (England), for "Victoria Station"; *Passage II* (anthology), for "For Three Days," "Grandparents in London," and "Wedding in Los Angeles"; *Passage III* (anthology), for "The Kiss" and "Night and Day" (from "Nocturne") and "View of Delft" (from "Three Young Men"); *Passage IV* (anthology), for "At Four Minutes to One"; *Passage V* (anthology), for "Herakleion: The Hidden Beach"—"Nocturne" an honors selection, all the other *Passage* poems prizewinners in the All Nations Poetry Contests for 1975, 1976, 1977, and 1978; *riverrun*, for "Gilbert and Sullivan Night at the Proms," "Macedonia," "Matilda," "The Pigeons of Maspeth," "Madrid: Coming Home," and "Sevilla: July 18th"; *Street*, for "Farewell to Crete"; *UCL Poetry 1969* (University of London anthology), for "A Girl's Funeral"; *Waves* (Canada), for "Crickets"; *Xanadu*, for "After the Poetry Reading," "Athens: Through Wide Open Shutters," "Dogs of San Miguel," "Nafplion: Snapshot," and "Thessaloniki: Three Sleeps"; *The Album* (Madras, India—anthology), for "Granada: The Rose"; and *Zagat: Jewish Life on New York's Lower East Side, 1912–1962*, for "Gimpl" (also excerpted in Irving Howe's *World of Our Fathers*). My special thanks to Charles Fishman, who not only selected these poems but whose sensitive and creative response has left its imprint on many of them.

Also to *Antigonish Review*, for "Breakfast" and "Down Escalator"; *Midstream*, for "Córdoba: Nocturne"; and *New England Review*, for "At Westminster Synagogue."

"Two Visits" appeared not in the discontinued *Modern Poetry Studies*, but in *Confrontation*. "Kennedy Airport" similarly appeared in *Midstream* instead, and is included in the 1980 *Anthology of American Magazine Verse*. The 1981 *Anthology* will include "Now, Before Shaving."

[7]

"But Here Was Form"
An Introduction by Charles Fishman

I

In the first half of Aaron Kramer's *Carousel Parkway and Other Poems*, the reader will find work that is centered in the poet's domestic life. Here there are poems that return us again and again to the crises all of us must face. Kramer's poems focus on the home, on family and friends, on what is near to the geographical center of our lives and, thus, immensely vulnerable. People are important to this poet who is not embarrassed by love; who is not a blasé sophisticate insulated from grief; who refuses to be hardened or broken, although the impact of a friend's death can be numbing; who will not allow himself to be emotionally neutered, although a man's inability to speak sagely for others when he himself is bereaved can seem an especially vicious form of emasculation. For Kramer, the past is never "buried." The memory of his dead father speaks to him with perhaps greater clarity and urgency than does the image of his new granddaughter—though the life just begun warms and reassures him and the life long since completed chills him and troubles him with its burden of longings unfulfilled. This tension between old and new allegiances is the subject of "Two Visits," "Gimpl," "Carousel Parkway," and a fair number of other poems. In "Carousel Parkway," in particular, the round of birth and death receives brilliant treatment. This is a poem in which Kramer has managed a summation of his principal themes: ghosts are encountered and laid to rest; relentlessly, one grows older, is ridden by grief, accepts the responsibility to mourn; slowly—and painfully—one grows stronger. All of these major chords are sounded within the framework of an architecturally and musically elegant poem.

For Kramer, anxiety is the face of change. The roar of a lion or the howl of a wolf is almost always just outside the door: the lion of painful losses, the wolf of voracious time. His poems confront the obscene ordinariness of daily life. We see this most clearly in poems like "Thanksgiving Day," where the poet ironically judges his own happiness in life against the physical and mental traumas suffered by colleagues, relatives, and friends, and "Softening," where we realize that the insidious change that has weakened the physical armor of a simple turtle is analogous to our own movements away from the protective "roof" of things well known and deeply loved. Kramer is always pausing in mid-stride, struck still and silent by a sudden ache of recognition. He feels himself beginning to walk like the old Jewish men in a hundred neighborhood parks. Behind every abandoned building, in the doorways of small cluttered shops, floating beneath the arching superstructures of a dozen spectacular bridges—ghosts, ghosts, a world filled with their unsettled arguments, their unsatisfied passions, their incontestable claims on the living.

Kramer is more at home with traditional "fixed" structures than are most of his contemporaries. "Closed" stanzaic forms, intricate rhyme schemes, richly textured patterns of sound—all of the old music is called upon to act as a "field" or "screen" against which this poet may project his deeply personal fears, failures, triumphs, visions. Yet Kramer usually addresses us in a modern idiom: he speaks as a well-traveled, complex, educated man; as professor and poet; as husband and father; as child of a young nation and scion of an old people . . . and he does not shy away from the troubled human self that informs each of these voices. Often, the tone we hear is both angry and confused, ironic and tender. In "Breakfast," for instance, we encounter the poet as he sits at the table one morning; his head is still cloudy with a welter of conflicting thoughts and impressions. A young man he knows is, apparently, quite ill; he understands, only too well, that a phone call should be made, that the seriousness of this crisis ought to take precedence over the demands of the body:

> As I heap my cereal,
> add banana to the hill,
> raisin-crown it, drown it under
> floods of milk and feast my fill,
> at each spoonful I grow humbler
> in the presence of his number.

Here the conscious man struggles to maintain his balance though assaulted by a wave of guilt he finds it impossible to control. The driving, obsessive force of the repeated variations of the key word "number" startles the reader. The scenario is mundane, so entirely familiar, yet the structure of the poem gives the lie to the surface tranquility. While Kramer devours his cereal-and-banana breakfast, his inner awareness of "Ronnie's" suffering gnaws at him, and the food he swallows sickens him, even as it sustains. Seventeen times, in a poem of thirty lines, the line breaks or stops on the sound that has become like a bell clanging in our ears: number, hunger, humbler, stronger, thunder, blunder.... The risk for the poet is very real. We might be deafened by this clangor, by this insistent and unappeasable call for our attention (and for his own); we might decide not to listen. But the music lifts us. Here, as so often elsewhere in his writing, the artistic and moral impact of Kramer's beautifully crafted poems will not permit us to turn away.

Kramer uses poetic structure, whether conventional or innovative, as a liberating element in his work. The strictly orchestrated form allows him to give shape to experiences and feelings that might otherwise prove impossible to delineate. He utilizes the sonnet's all-but-too-recognizable pattern, its complex prosodic demands, to express varying but intense moods: "The Month Is Ripening," "Down Escalator," "Sunset," "Glasses." Each poem succeeds in moving us, drawing us into its carefully defined world. But there is another sonnet in this first section of the book that is especially worthy of our study. In "A Girl's Funeral," Kramer's handling of the sonnet form is truly masterful and surprising:

> The death was a crashing, indefensible zigzag
> disrupting currents of rivers, twisting mileposts.
> Friends of my youth became puppets in masks and wigs, a
> greedy, groan-lapping pack....

Note how the diction of these swirling, plunging lines echoes Kramer's confusion and disdain. The rabbi's eulogy, pro forma and safely distant from honest indignation, is a "comfortless drool"; the funeral they must drive to is a "dunging of beauty."

[11]

The forced "feminine" rhymes, the jolting and shifting rhythms, are the poet's shorthand, mocking the sterile, smooth-toned, even-tempered ritualizations of grief. These rhymes—zigzag/wigs ag (the final "g" sound is grafted onto the rhyme from the initial consonant in the succeeding line), rabbi/cab by—are awkwardly difficult twistings of language. The mouth, lips, jaw must work at forming them; the face contorts; the mind registers the energy expended. In the sestet, however, Kramer discovers a center for his turbulent feelings, a series of eloquently interrelated curves and planes—a figure—powerful enough to bring this chaos to heel:

> I suddenly found, unengulfed by the doorway swarm,
> a girl and a boy: ashen, transfixed, mute, he
> having learned to become for her fluttering a cocoon.
> The wildness had frozen my tears; but here was form.

"But here was form" is just right: two perfect iambs, feeling given form, form in the service of truth. In "A Girl's Funeral," the sonnet's carefully molded structure—a centering "cocoon"—is the poet's lens that holds the wild sensations in. Here, as so frequently in his best work, Kramer retrieves for us what we have almost ceased to look for in modern poetry: the joining of high moral vision to significant, purposeful form. Whether the shape of his stanzas is traditional and familiar—as in "Matilda" or sections of "Carousel Parkway"—or idiosyncratic and original, as in the hauntingly lyrical elegy for his friend, Arthur Kevess ("The Pigeons of Maspeth"), Kramer manages this rarest manifestation of poetic artistry.

II

The second part of *Carousel Parkway* has been given to a selection of Kramer's travel poems. Here we discover that Kramer is a voyager, a citizen of the world. Whereas many of his contemporaries seem content to write poems that loosely embody a regional character, Kramer has consistently attempted to capture in his work the very essence of a shared human history. He is entranced by that dazzling but, too often, wretched caravan. The past lives for him: the spilled blood and poverty of a Mexican town are real to him; the churches, palaces, bazaars and shrines—and, yes, the cemeteries—of Europe are visited as if each worn stone were sacred, as if their histories were his.

Unlike Ruskin or Irving or Twain, who could—in each instance—assume that the architectural or geographical or historical landmarks they described would be important news for a populace largely rooted to home ground, the jet-lag writer who journeys at supersonic speeds to exotic ports, though he records his perceptions with charm and fidelity, has no such assurances. Most of his peers will have already made their grand or little tours of the old world and the new; and what has not actually been visited will often have been paraded—as the location for the latest "TV movie" or James Bond thriller—before the same eyes that will read his stories or poems. Pound's mandate to "Make it new" must now extend to descriptions of museums and houses of parliament, to ancient monuments and once unreachable beaches. The sand of the overly familiar has been kicked into our eyes. Kramer meets this challenge with great skill and immense energy. He shows us the stones of a tower we have all but lived in, and we see them clearly for the first time; he focuses his attention on the market place, or the hotel room, or the proverbial village square—and we acquiesce to his vision. He makes these row houses of the known, these names nearly ruined for us by the glaring sameness of ads in the Sunday Travel Section, glimmer again with a patina of age and mystery. And he shows us a few things we may have missed. His "View of Delft" is not likely to have been our own, nor is his account of a near-confrontation with the Muse at Delphi or his stunning evocation of Italian history in "Piazza del Campidoglio" similar to any other tale we are likely to have been told of such wonders.

Kramer always displays the human face of the worlds he comes to as tourist, as seeker. He is caught up in the "sensual music," though (as in the tender and moving "Grandparents in London" or the humorous and much bolder "Journal Entry" or the plaintive "Geneve Lobby") Kramer does find himself temporarily buffeted by the whims of bureaucrats, shipwrecked by missed appointments, half-drowned by outbursts of weather. Such downpours of bad luck can jade the most stalwart of travelers and it is to his credit that Kramer transforms them into the stuff of poems. In these masterful creations, he breaks through the egocentricity of the experience to reveal the essential spirit of a nation, to record this faithfully, to find the ghosts of another time and bring them back to life. Consider the abrupt, explosive opening stanza of "Westminster Synagogue":

> Ears afire, I knock at Kent House door.
> My hands could not protect them if I tried
> except from the drone of Heathrow jets, the roar
> of a bus marked "Kensington." Too deep inside,
> the tick of an Irish bomb at Harrod's store,
> the swords forever committing chivalricide
> athwart Knightsbridge, the million-footed squall
> from Victoria's trains to Exhibition Hall.

In passages such as this, it can be seen that, while he will frequently refer to the usual markers of guidebook history, Kramer is not content unless he uses such data for a higher purpose. His poems are never merely catalogues, though their concreteness and particularity are built upon a foundation of authentic history and observed fact.

Here are several excerpts from "The Last Supper," an unstintingly honest and vividly wrought canvas, from which Kramer addresses us as the Jesus of da Vinci's great painting:

> Who but Leonardo could conjure me onto his wall,
> choosing, of all traumatic moments, my very worst?

> Years he wrought, till even he was satisfied
> it really was I who sat there
> central amid the apostles, tranquil-faced
> while storming them with my charge of betrayal.

> By Borromeo's time I was so far gone,
> the Cardinal ordered a copy made;
> and when Torre in 1674 sighed "Lost!"
> I, half-reascended already,
> could hardly restrain my lips from an alleluia.

> Then it began: two centuries of crucifixion....

The conclusion, which involves a necessary and dramatic shift of perspective, is typical of Kramer's point of view:

—Thus move the pale lips of the Christ.
But his story takes too long.
As he gauges the agitation of his followers,
a Japanese couple peer at a map of the city . . . .

Here Kramer enumerates the distractions which draw him away from the painting. We share with him the intensity of his immersion in the masterpiece, in this artifact that is itself a window into an earlier, still more turbulent, age. We have been made witnesses to a deeply symbolic, highly charged scenario that wounds us and taunts us, that pulls us—relentlessly—into the circle of its power. And, finally, we are forced to let the moment go. The crush of the crowd wakes us from our trance, the click of the omnipresent tourist camera snaps us out of our daydream, our encounter with the past.

It is this last element—what Kramer calls "our predatory lens"—that is most disturbing to the poet. He uses the Kodak instamatic as a metaphor for all that separates life from art, experience from rumination, immediacy from self-conscious craft. The lens of the camera—our modern, civilized window through which we peer at the lives and relics we "purchase" with our plane tickets—narrows the field of vision for the lens of the eye. The paradox, which Kramer intuitively recognizes (see, for instance, the resolution to "Herakleion"), is that this same lens may also sharpen that vision and help to preserve it. Similarly, the lens of the poem distorts what the mind's eye only half remembers, yet may capture and illuminate significant fragments of place, time, action, belief, and mood, which are, in truth, the essential component of our history.

III

Aaron Kramer is, before all else, a man of deep feelings. His memory is long, his instincts are acute, his moral energies are engaged. Kramer's poetry is never frivolous or obtuse; he is not a propagandist for every modish cause; his voice is not computerized, pre-packaged, laundered, prettied-up; his concerns are not dictated by the dull priorities of the age. Instead, we confront in Kramer's poetry a survival of the old music; in his best poems, clearly conceived ideas are presented with consummate skill and unaffected passion. Kramer has a muse—he has drunk deeply, has been drunk with poetry and life. His poems memorialize the victims of a violent and dehumanizing past; but they also honor the many victories of the creative human spirit that have helped to keep us whole and sane and vital through the dizzying spiral of centuries. Kramer shows us the small deaths that forever alter our understanding of ourselves; and he gives us the triumphs over despair and boredom and the dark fires of the soul. His voice is marked by high seriousness and biting wit, by brooding anger and genuine compassion. His is a fiercely accurate pen that has been dipped boldly and faithfully into the lifeblood of this world.

Notes

1. "Piazza del Campidoglio"
   Dany the Red—French radical youth leader during the 1968 upsurge.
   FUAN—initials of a neo-Fascist youth organization
   Marcus Aurelius—The emperor's benign statue on horseback was
      excavated many centuries after the conquering Goths hurled it into
      the Tiber, and restored to the piazza, overlooking the Colosseum
      and Forum.
   Rienzi—a fourteenth-century popular leader of Rome.
   Tarpeian Rock—a steep cliff at one side of the Capitol, down which in
      ancient times "enemies" of Rome were hurled (see *Coriolanus*).
2. "Sevilla"
   "at five in the dying day"—the first line of Lorca's masterpiece, "Lament
      for the Death of a Bullfighter."
   barrio—neighborhood.
   "But to the girdle do the gods inherit . . ."—*King Lear* (IV, 6, 128–31).
   Colón—Columbus.
   Giralda—the popular name of Seville's cathedral.
   Guardia Incivil—Lorca's last great poem describes the Civil Guard's
      murderous night raid on Granada's gypsy quarter; the Civil Guard
      avenged themselves for this ballad by murdering the poet on the
      night of August 5, 1936.
   Santa Cruz—Formerly the Jewish quarter, this is Seville's most
      picturesque and popular tourist area.
3. "Córdoba"
   Gabirol, the poet, and *Maimonides*, the philosopher—among Córdoba's
      greatest Jews of the Golden Age.
   Lucan, the poet, and *Seneca*, the dramatist—among the outstanding
      figures of classical Latin literature, both born in Córdoba.
4. "Granada"
   Acera del Casino—Lorca's street, just off the Puerta Real and across from
      the Avenida Jose Antonio.
   Albaicin—Lorca's favorite section of Granada, the only old quarter spared
      by Isabel and Fernando when they demolished Moorish Granada
      and drove out the Moslems.
   Isabel ("the Catholic") and *Fernando*—ruled Castile jointly from 1474 to
      1504; they celebrated the conquest of Granada by building a great
      cathedral there, and beside it a pretentious chapel destined to house
      their remains.
   José Antonio—Falangist leader for whom major streets and squares are
      named, and whose statue appears in many cities, including Granada
      (across from Lorca's window).
   Valdes—the Commandante in charge of Lorca's murder.

I
Carousel Parkway

THANKSGIVING DAY

He was unready to get out of bed,
let alone give thanks.
Yesterday
the cup had jumped
out of his hand,
and he'd dumped
a lump of margarine
instead of its wrapper
into the garbage.
Yesterday his joints had ached,
and his back,
though not dramatically enough
to mention at breakfast.
Yesterday's sun had set
like one's life, slowly,
behind the vulnerable trees
that resembled his friends.

It was only when he remembered them
that thanks rose
poisoningly
into his skull.
He was thankful
not to be Florence
whose cancer (probably) was caught in time;
Jack, who would never again
meet Lily at museum doors;
Fred, pacing the deathways of San Francisco
for a glimpse of his daughter;
Victor, ebbing without witnesses
in a germproof room;
Harriet, head awry,
as if snapped by the paw
of a dinosaur, triumphant
over nothing but her scream.

NOW, BEFORE SHAVING

The blanket loosens.
But if she comes in, I'll pretend to be sleeping.
I'd rather not make orange juice,
slice fruit into cereal,
seek out the darkest suit
and argue which tie goes best with it.
I'd rather not promise to fetch home as trophies
a hospital's name,
its autopsy chart.
I'd rather not have the mortuary pinpointed on a street map,
my scene with the widow coached.
I'd rather not hear from a metal box it will be sunny all day.

To have fallen asleep without five minutes of mourning!
Now, before shaving, I want to see us
at college, the cafeteria group;
our Washington reunion, the Mellon Gallery concert;
home from war, still in uniform at that crazy party;
weddings, housewarmings;
New Year's Eves in the finished basement,
his improvised deadpan dance, lifting a partner in air;
The Merchant of Venice at Stratford,
disputing Carnovsky in Shylock's dressing room
over Shakespeare's intentions,
driving home the excitement, keeping it up till four,
spilling it over through brunch the next day;
our first quarrel: Israel, the Arabs;
a misfired phone call, declined invitations,
rumors of a musician son, an architect daughter,
his name in the paper once,
an unmailed note.

Now, before shaving, is the time to feel.
Three friends buried in three months' time
and a feel not of heartache so much as cold feet.
The blanket's come loose, I lie at the edge of a sea,

[22]

the tide covers my toes, my ankles.
She comes in, fixes the blanket,
but there is no time.
A drowned face waits at the mirror.

BREAKFAST

It is almost half past eight
and I wonder
what my sleeping late
has to do with Ronnie's number.
On the kitchen table wait
bowl, plate,
Ronnie's number.
Ronnie, please forgive my great
morning hunger.
As I heap my cereal,
add banana to the hill,
raisin-crown it, drown it under
floods of milk and feast my fill,
at each spoonful I grow humbler
in the presence of his number.
Something else should have been stronger
than my hunger—
for the pulse that once was thunder
barely murmurs back at mine
though it's twenty-one years younger;
and the voice that was a wonder
barely whispers on the line
—as I'll learn at five to nine
when I dial Ronnie's number
and he will not say he's fine
and I won't so much as mumble
please forgive my morning hunger;
please forgive the morning's blunder,
that, instead of roars of thunder
raging down, the sun can shine.

UNCLE

Something deserves to be said.
Yesterday morning he was alive,
by afternoon he was dead.
He *was* the last of five
to bid the Poland of our grandparents goodbye.
My features *do* resemble
his: broad nose, green eye.
His life
did crumble
year by year behind the crumbling store:
a deafmute son, a shrewish wife
against whom in each letter he would pour
his gall out, till she died
—then pined as if she'd been a three-hours bride.
He *was* an early reject from
the world of trade:
kenneled, grateful for whatever crumb
a daughter-in-law delivered to the shade
of his cold basement
where, coughing thanks, he froze and burned
by turns, and gradually learned
what having neither name nor face meant.

I believe
all this, repeat
all this, in order to begin to grieve.
Maybe by tomorrow tears will mingle with my meat.

BELLA

They have weighed my suitcases, but I carry
something more into the plane.

Day after day, across two desks,
Bella faced me: entrenched
in her beauty, her politics, and her British accent.
Five years later the beauty was shot,
and with it her marriage
(though which was cause and which effect
I could never be sure).
Then out leaked the zeal
like fluid out of a battery.
What faced me, against its will, in the hospital
was a battered, unmanned shell,
not the flag-flying Bella of old
—nothing left but her doggedly East End speech.

She'd boarded her mangy trophies with our dentist,
who had room to spare in his basement,
and in his X-ray file the slowly rotting
history of her teeth.

At last the fact made ready: the coiled, patient fact.
Having learned I was in San Francisco,
it slithered to the party.
On an innocuous tray,
among anchovies and liver,
it let itself be carried straight across the room.

And until I have opened my mouth
in the dentist's office
wide, wider than he asks me to—
until I have set it free and cloven it,
half for him, half for me—
I shall stoop, though the blind admire my posture,
under the venomous pounds of Bella's suicide.

[25]

GLASSES

Six cocktail glasses—gaudy as the cousin
who thrust them on us several housewarmings back—
glower on the shelf, infernally half a dozen:
none stained or faded, none with a chip or a crack.

If curses could, if looks could murder glass,
not one would now be alive; and they *are* living—
they *must* be: why else would a wife harass
them year after year with eyes that are unforgiving?

The deaths of cherished persons make one think
that maybe prayer should be abandoned, maybe
caresses and medicines should be replaced
by a wife's way: let grandmother, let baby
be slammed with a glare, a curse into the sink
and washed, dried, shoved on a narrow shelf in haste.

A GIRL'S FUNERAL

The death was a crashing, indefensible zigzag
disrupting currents of rivers, twisting mileposts.
Friends of my youth became puppets in masks and wigs, a
greedy, groan-lapping pack. Up, down the aisle ghosts
ran, obscenely gesturing, as from the rabbi
a comfortless drone lipped forth—that once was language.
Soon the bewildered were shown to a sable cab by
the flawlessly professional chauffeurs of anguish.

But before our drive to that chaos—that dunging of beauty—
those fingernail-shrieks skinning the face of noon—
I suddenly found, unengulfed by the doorway swarm,
a girl and a boy: ashen, transfixed, mute, he
having learned to become for her fluttering a cocoon.
The wildness had frozen my tears; but here was form.

MATILDA

Behind, in rows, her cousins sat,
her husband, sons, a brother,
with dozens more whose murmured chat
and clustered nod gave notice that
each mourner knew the other.

All hushed, however, when I stood
before her at the coffin,
as if my gaze might change her mood—
so deep estranged—might wake the blood
and make the features soften.

And so I watched a painful while
her lips, but never made them
so much as simulate a smile.
Back through her kin I crawled. The aisle
was long. I had betrayed them.

FOR THREE DAYS

Although they packed her into the car
and turned the corner
and she had no idea where she was going,
and for three days she poked 'round our nooks and noses
and had no idea who we were,
and now they've repacked her,
turned the corner,
and she has no idea why, or whereto, or when if ever she'll be back
—it's happening already:

already I hear her in my converted study,
hands gripping the crib-side
like a pilot in a storm,
urged on by Pushkin, Homer, Keats,
her morning-roar outsoaring them;
already I see her at the living-room pane
absorbing, utterly still, the wind-seized oak,
then, with head, arms, lips,
trying its dance, its zhhhizzzh.

Every room, in fact—even the bathroom
where last night in the tub,
drenched hair pasted down,
she sailed her unwearying duck,
and the kitchen, whose forbidden drawer,
the one with knives,
held her, a pirate-apprentice, for three days—
every room quakes with her presence,
aches with her absence.

Perhaps it is best they take her far;
perhaps it is best they will not soon return.
I have done my time, have survived that madness;
I might not be able to stand the terrors
of another such love:
night after night waking in a cold sweat

from that vision I never dared relate, even to my wife,
of our girls crisscrossing canyons on cobwebs
followed by me, arms out, the scream locked in.

SUNSET

Half the west! from Coney to Mount Vernon!
in the seconds before I realize
that it's not the neighborhoods of New York turning
the skies red, but they turned red by the skies
—tenements split, splinter; flame enjoys
a bridge's neckbone; Brooklyn College is burning;
Mephisto sings at the Met; library eyes
out-Dante 42nd Street's inferno.

Ciphers writhing . . . insect arms afire . . .
Please! let a wrong wind not blow it nearer!
—But suddenly, faces in the hive glow clearer,
among them my own child's!! And I perspire
at the wheel, press hard the gas, desire
to dial her number, hear it ringing, hear her . . . .

THE PIGEONS OF MASPETH
for Arthur Kevess

Behind me, past Manhattan, past Morphia Island,
the sun was dropping, without a struggle,
into the uncouth jaws of Hoboken and Weehawken.
Ahead of me Long Island held up a great gray banner
as well it might.

I was glad to be driving alone,
uncompelled to be civil, to blaspheme with small talk
the passing of Arthur.
Bad enough that my stomach leaned toward the coming meal,
that my nerves slashed back at the surge
of radio news and traffic.
I wanted to focus entirely on the wasted face and frame,
the forthright confession of envy that I could move freely
while he lay pinned to his fate, to his bones, to his bed,
with power only to raise his torso by pressing a button
and then in a restless rage to lower it.

Suddenly beyond the windshield
a fireworks blossom burst—and another, another—
till five recurrent clusters of sparkles
flung their statement against the gray.
Fireworks! What ghoul was on the prowl,
making a holiday of Arthur's passing?
But no. These were no fireworks. Five companies of pigeons,
reprieved from the roofs of Maspeth,
were doing their dance, their soundless song,
and at one certain instant during every gyration
the sunset wand transformed them
into five fireworks blossoms.

Perhaps they had flung themselves so
into other dusks, and would again—
perhaps each burst was of joy at being loose in the wind
or of panic at the sun their god's decline.

[30]

But not to me;
for all at once I was privileged
to be sitting again by the bed, a witness,
as Arthur, ever-gentle, and now altogether strengthless Arthur,
gathered unto himself—for one last act of defiance—
a power like Prometheus', pinned to his rock,
torn by the beaks of furies;
and I saw that every luminous turning of those wingéd things
was Arthur's spirit, unbroken in the broken body,
breaking loose from the ninth, the terminal floor:
clutching his forehead, complaining that I made him think,
then, for an hour, between seizures of agony and thirst,
punning, rhyming, explaining the nature of his condition,
responding to my "Well, dear friend, I must be getting on the
            highway,"
with a long handclasp, a wisp of grin,
and then, to help his children smile,
a "Both of us must go—you on the highway,
and I...soon...on the potty."

This was Arthur's final prose. The fireworks were his final poem.
Driving into dusk,
that day and from now on,
the pigeons of Maspeth stood and will stand for his spirit
turning its clean breast, its broad wingspan,
for yet one more reflection—or, better, one more contradiction—
of the sun that, without a struggle,
had almost dropped from sight.

PREMONITIONS

Her voice named him softly;
but no—no one stood near.
    Is this the way for older men
    in tropic shopping malls, on benches,
    who start and look toward the revolving doors
    through which their wives once burst?

Later, unconvinced by the motel film,
he waited flat on a wide bed
while laughter, animated zoris
runneled past the drapes
toward lawn-play, gaily steaming pool.
    Is this the way for older men
    who start at the provocative
    ghost-song of the shower
    from which their wives once stepped?

This year they are everywhere
and this their way:
    taking the old route,
    finding the old table,
    dozing, till the ghost mouth grinds again:
    Why is there always too much on your spoon?
    till those phantom eyes of concentrated scorn
    blaze once more at flap-mad jacket pocket,
    mismatched tie and shirt.

DOWN ESCALATOR

Was it all in the cards, the leaves, the crystal ball?
Had I not lost thirty pounds that year, would *my*
remains be boxed in a bomber lost near the Pole,
no daughter to lead a conference come July?

Had I phoned the placement office one day after,
would someone else have taken the job eight miles
past the bridge, *his* passenger Mabel's laughter
fading, name soon buried in the files?

Had I reached Macy's fifth floor escalator
seconds before, would someone else have read
the salesclerk's sidelong glance, craving to date her,
and caught her upturned, downward floating head:
"How was your birthday?" and beheld him lift
an arm to flash the bulova, the gift?

AFTER THE POETRY READING

Sure enough, she's sleeping
—just as the two had predicted.
Zigzagging through the darkness
I guessed as much myself.

The car's old motor rattled,
as mine did, older still.
It was serious—we should have
pulled over, somewhere, and rested.

And what if she weren't sleeping?
Would she let herself mutter
"How did it go?" I doubt
my "Very well" would please her.

And, really, they weren't as bad
as some of the poets I've dealt with,
though the boy took praise like a princeling
and the woman heard herself only.

Quietly I undress,
quietly nest beside her.
We are faced away from each other,
our buttocks barely touching.

Not to be at the table
in the rear of the Chinese tearoom
slowly begins to please me
though, sure enough, she sleeps.

NIGHT AND DAY

1.

When I climb between the bedclothes in the night
and brush against the body of my wife,
a twittering starts within me: Rest,
old bird, still safe in the nest.

2.

My wife turned on the ignition;
she was out the driveway and gone;
it took me an hour to get out of bed
and stand on the planet alone.

NOCTURNE

Here on the Island at 10:15 rain fingers the roof
gently but more distinctly now that she turns the tv off.
It's 9:15 in Chicago; the wind's a prowling wolf
window by window, room by room, finding no sign of wife.
Mine asks me to unzip her gown, hands me some ointment stuff;
across the shoulder blades, along the spine, what's dry and rough
sings at my touch, and at the touch my manhood springs to life.
Tonight her hand clutched his, her eyes clutched his—a word, a
              cough.
    Wordless under the warm electric blanket with a laugh
she lets me pull her, wordless under kisses clear enough
but never enough, once again one, half unto half,
once again clock-proof, once again rain-proof, Chicago-proof
—till under all three we suddenly lie prone as under the knife
at 7 tomorrow morning she plans to surrender herself
—spine, shoulder blade, anything else desired by staff, by graph—
as under the frosty blanket he crawls at last, his manhood stiff
in the clutch of the chill, in the laugh of the wind, whose word's an
              epitaph.

[35]

THE KISS

Let her think it passion only,
but also a shadow
tough as a tomb door
rives her lips from mine.

Instead of praising
the kiss of thirty years
I press, press toward her—
privately cursing

as if we were the cheated
children of Verona
riven after
their consummation rite:

would thirty years have made them
less pale that dawn,
his ladder less
like a passage into the ground?

—and I, would I answer
after a Zeus-long marriage
with less indignant lips
the riving shadow?

CRICKETS

After they broke from each other's breathing,
he learned how large a choir of crickets
had lifted their voices at nightfall in one high
trill that continued and would continue
till dawn. It was taut as a high-tension wire
on which one must never dare lay a finger;
taut as a string section seized by hysteria
knowing the trumpets' intention; taut as
his veins, and striking precisely the note his
blood would if it could. He lay there listening
to that long shriek as if to himself.

RAIN

Long in labor, only now,
bedding my page down, do I hear
a rain that started hours ago;
and as I prepare
my self for bed, though a sweet fullness rounds me
—like the calmly singing clock
in the kitchen, where
bottle, nipple soak—
though a fresh dream finds me
from the den, behind whose door
my grandchild hibernates,
from the guest room down the corridor
where my daughter and her mate
doze with the tv on,
from the bed toward which I burrow,
where my wife breathes the half-sigh, half-moan
I alone and long have known,
—a dread corrodes my marrow
as the sound of rain corrodes my house:
a hollow sound
as if my rooms no longer were in use,
as if my page were compost in the ground,
as if my self were creeping without hope of sleep
toward a haunted pillow, toward phantom hair and lip.

SOFTENING

It was then I remembered
how cold in my hand once huddled
a turtle which had not budged for days
from his miserable bit of rock.

His shell had softened;
his vividness seemed to have run;
his eyes ignored my compassion;
the concept of lettuce had grown terribly remote;
water, as a way of life, was finished;
still and stiller he became,
introverted unto death.

And I wondered
about the very start of it:
was it by virus or decision?
a metabolic
or a philosophic collapse?
sudden or slow?
required of the genus
or quite subjective, individual?
on a day too bright and warm, while the family laughed,
or a night too dark and cold, while we were dreaming?

Especially the softness I remembered,
the softness of the shell.

ATTICA IN THE SUBURBS

1. *Nightfall*

You had chosen windows
across from the round-rail fence
on which, like a hitchhiker,
leaned the rose vine.
But with one chew
night polished off the fence
as if it were bread
and the roses rode away
on noiseless wheels.

2. *At the TV Set*

That night in September
she knew she'd been taken.
When brickwork nor plaster
nor guarantee proffered
by real estate agent,

nor cricket, nor murmur
of maple succeeded
in keeping out "brother,"
that night in September
she knew she'd been cheated.

That night in September
she knew she'd been had
when miles did not matter,
when rage roared around her
in Attica yard.

3. *The Coming*

They have found the way.
They've cut through the counties,
spanned the rivers,
reached the milepost,
and left the highway.
They move past the stop sign
without one glance
at the deli neon.
They are neither in graves
nor in solitary
nor in the far prisons
to which they were transferred;
but, knit together
as in those five days,
they come like a fist
around the corner.
What do they want?
All right, they can have it!
My friend's round-rail fence?
No, they have passed it
without one glance
at the hitchhiker rose vine
leaning against it.
They cross to my mailbox.
They crowd my window.
Their mouths become craters.
They want my eyes.

THE MONTH IS RIPENING

The month is ripening toward a funeral.
All must be there now. Ringed as if to recover
a failing flame by conjuration, they hover
around their heap of ash whose spark, grown small,
apologizes that once again they must all
be there now, that it takes so long to be over,
that here is no longer the father, the friend, the lover,
but a failing flame magic cannot recall.

The phone rings. Not yet. It is not them yet.
A merry voice, a far-fetched voice, rolls in;
arrangement is made to meet some hour somewhere.
A day passes. Doing our chores we forget.
But through the window at midnight comes a thin
whimper of wind. All must now be there.

FOREBODINGS

Nowadays I'm shaken by forebodings.
A ripe-looking tomato has no taste
and I imagine kids
snickering at old folks' efforts
to describe like a myth
the experience of a sweet red slice.

I drowse in the daytime, am drawn
to the couch, and I imagine
that this is how it begins:
the big sleep overpowering us
joint by joint, month by month.

At night in the wind
all the world's trees,
beginning deep in the woods
till they reach my very own oak,
raise their voices
in one sustained primeval note

and I imagine them
in a time that is coming
roused to such outcry, such lamentation,
joined by the voice of neither beast nor man,
heard neither by devil nor god.

GIMPL

Bloodless, aching
after a day at the machine,
it was for Gimpl he gave his child the coin,
for Gimpl his child skipped to the newsstand
and fetched home *Warheit*,
for Gimpl Beinish, the busybody,
the bearded little matchmaker
with beady eyes,
rushing off to the beach, the park, the Catskills,
any likely place of mating,
for Gimpl Beinish, who in yesterday's cartoon
had miserably flopped,
but, self-propelled,
was surely on the trail again,
unleashed by his creator, "Z,"
burying his initial
in a corner of the comic strip.

Where now is "Z"?
Ashes on Long Island.
And where that immigrant,
coughing, guffawing over Gimpl
six flights down the East Side airshaft?
A name in a crowded row these thirty years.
His child, surviving still another winter,
crawls toward the sunrays of the benches.
His grandchildren, graying in the suburbs,
wonder what matches their boys and girls make
in far-off colleges.

And Gimpl, the busybody,
bursting with energy, with hope,
Gimpl waits
for the slightest signal
to tear loose from the microfilm of 1912
and range the globe, self-propelled
in search of prospects.

MR. GLICKLICH TAKES A SHOWER

Who thought of thanking
whirlwind committees,
tornado weekends,
volcano children?

Now that silence
seeps through every crack,
he finds himself thankful
for nails that need cutting,
bowels too empty or full,
a chair ready for reupholstery,
a hospitalized friend,
evening.

Evening still comes.
Once more he straightens out the bathmat,
chooses washcloth and towel,
prepares robe and slippers,
adjusts the flow,
steps in.

Then, suddenly, it happens:
eyes shut, taking it full force,
feeling it hammer through
veins, lungs, intestines,
he stands in a world
that has only water.

He is thirty-four, circling Garda,
guzzling in his thirst its Giotto blue;
he is twenty-four, wheeling his baby
to the fountain in Washington Square;
he is fourteen, repaying spray with madrigals
the length of Gravesend Bay;
he is four, above the shadowy Hudson,
on a mountainside across from Newburgh,
joining his mouth to the nipple of a spring;

he is the first breather ever cradled by the sea;
he is the seagod.

Drying himself, combing the seaweed out,
he steps forth
prepared with sturdy strokes
to try whatever deeps.

CONEY ISLAND

By day your approach to Coney Island
may be what it may be—rounding the road
at sixty an hour, high-rise apartments
blocking the boardwalk, the parachute ride;
by night you approach on foot, no nickel
for trolley, Gowanus a timeless moat,
its deep putrescence guarding the savor
of sea; orgasmic spurts of delight
and terror blend as the roller-coaster
plunges or turns; a pride of puffed
pandas ignore the line of ascetic,
one-dimensional ducks that drift
dreaming themselves the swans of Tschaikowsky
while slowly a rifle is lifted and aimed;
the dwarf, the titan, the bearded lady,
the man with breasts, stand forth proclaimed
as if at auction (for adults only),
while under the boardwalk, in mothering shade,
perfect bodies pair, unwitnessed
except by eyes that are new and wide;

and seized for worship, seized by the gleaming
teacup stare of a rouge-round face,
in through his leer, in through his barrel
of fun, toward strange selves at the glass
you crawl; and the waves, the purple stallions,
roll, and you straddle one of them: now
it dies, and icily its phantom
suggests in an undertone: *Let go . . .*,
and you leap-frog, wing over friends (including
five not yet shot out of the sky),
and all the mothers, full-haired, full-throated,
chant (in a tongue then alive, as were they).

By day your backward glance through the mirror
may be what it may be—galloping past
Gravesend Bay; by night, to the highest
roof you climb for a fireworks feast
year after year, unslaked, unsated,
devouring each preposterous bloom
(but also once, in a thrill of pity,
you gaped at Coney Island aflame—
two miles off, on a bench with cronies,
snacking on rumors of ladies and gents
who staggered away past the leer of the fungod,
on fire, without even underpants,
dimensional ducks who dreamed of Tschaikowsky
till fate like a rifle caused them to dance
with only the littlest bathhouse towel
covering up their fronts).

KENNEDY AIRPORT

Those greetings! those goodbyes!
I am passing Kennedy Airport—would know it blindfold
by the glad snarl of jets.
Many times, living near, we told each other:
One night, let's take off and arrive
with those great dragons!
Let's watch some families
go through their griefs, their joys!
Now the terminals are blended in my head,
and our passengers—going, coming—and the years;
arrivals too late, departures too early,
meeting places botched,
fragile names blared like hospital personnel . . .
only the pattern is clear:
children wrenched away, and again, again,
wrenched away, after each crumb of a visit,
to Chicago, Ann Arbor, finally Kermanshah,
our noses rubbed in the fact, again and again,
that they were not part of the unit any more,
that the nest was down to two . . .
and other arrivals, other departures,
always with huggings, tears;
always a clutching, not a clasping of hands.

I cannot pass Kennedy Airport without aching,
though for us it means greetings as well as goodbyes
—unlike my grandmother, she who coughed forth her soul
in the back of a wagon alone
on her way to a doctor too late
on a snow-cursed Polish road
without a goodbye from her husband
(but greeted by God at least, I would like to believe);
unlike my grandmother, who never did make it to America
where I hoped all my young years to greet her,
and who never even came to the depot
on those five nightmare mornings
as her children were wrenched away,

goodbye after goodbye,
depot with no greetings, only goodbyes,
till her nest was down to two,
without ever one telephone syllable to breathe or receive,
one word to decipher or place on a postcard;
waiting, waiting for the steerage tickets
her five American children and their mates
never did grow quite prosperous enough to send.

GHOSTS

1.

Because they are sponsorless and shy,
five years—even ten—go by
before some of my ghosts receive
mysterious privilege: reprieve.

2.

Aunts who enfolded me, baked for me, played with my name,
uncles who lifted me, questioned me, gave me pennies:
once I knew the smell and touch of your foyers;
once you starred in my dreams and expectations;
now, with an ache that awakes me, I greet your gliding
entrance, aunt with hairy mole on the chin,
uncle with flashy tie, upcurled moustache.

3.

Sometimes in the deep of night
I find myself in the bathroom
clutching my forehead.
But I don't need a pill.
It's not my blood pressure.
It's the bloodless pressure
of too many ghosts.

They seem to empty through my bladder.
After that I can sleep.
What will be in a year or two
I am afraid to think.
Maybe one night my skull will burst outright,
or become so loaded
I'll begin to double forward when I walk
like my old neighbors
on their way to the benches.
If I, with only fifty years of phantoms,
must fight to hold my head up,
imagine them at seventy-five!
In hours of bench-talk, I suppose,
a few ghosts float through their lips
out into the air.
This lightens them a little.
They manage to crawl home to dinner.

4.

It is not so much
because I have you at my mercy,
because you counted on me
and I let you down;
it is because
even the most respected ghosts
huddle like beasts in a stall
or slaves in the hold of a ship
unable even to beg for air;
and I see myself soon enough
among you
awaiting my moment
in the dream of a middle-aged daughter.

Carousel Parkway

I

1. Bridgeward

It was a simple route.
We had made it often enough before:
eighty-seven and a half miles, door to door.
We were coming to salute
our Jersey daughter on her birthday, big with child—
the traffic reasonable, the weather mild.

Because this unborn would be someone I wanted to live to see,
I kept my eyes on the road
though Brooklyn's waters beckoned me,
my old beloved bays, that glowed
in pre-noon sun, and ultimately the Bridge,
built long past my time, but fixed as if endlessly there,
or, poised as a rested fire-drake—inspired—about to cleave the air
on its own Sunday pilgrimage.

2. The Hat

What with the lilt of Von Suppè's
Boccaccio duets I'd never heard till then;
what with the rays
that ricochet from needles only when
a grandmother crochets
a unisex green hat;
what with our chat
on grandsires' proper conduct and much else
in the same vein, I scarcely noticed that
we'd left the Island parkway and were now
wheeling around the one that belts
Brooklyn and Queens. Oh yes, somehow
out of the corner of my eye
I saw familiar entrances and exit signs rush by
swift as a lifetime in the mind
of one about to die;
but soon they fell behind;
two rivers and a state line lay between
my vague past and the future toward whose readying room
my wife's lap, a humming loom,
hurried her half-done hat of green.

3. Home

Later, on those eighty-seven and a half
homecoming miles, full of our daughter's birthday meal,
full of the new flesh I could almost feel
now that I knew what name it soon would have,
I noticed neither the entrance avenue that had been mine
lulled by the Canarsie Line
nor my father's exit sign
where bones and epitaph
slowly soften in the rains.

And, lying down that night, why should I hear the Brownsville
        trains
that long had rockabied me?
Why should the February of my father's death
once more heap the snows inside me?
—Full of the blood beginning in my grandchild's veins,
full of the breath
about to fill its lung,
full of the melody soon to roll off its tongue,
I fell asleep with *my* new song:
Andrew . . . Nora Elizabeth . . . .

4. Mixed Dream

Past the top landing and out the roof door,
through the next roofway and past the top floor,
gingerly bearing as often before
something of magic;

hushed in the hallway, a hand on the knob,
while from within comes a song or a sob:
"Sleep and grow hardy; someday, Little Bob,
you'll be important!"

lovingly noticed and called by my name,
proffering proudly, when asked why I came,
marvelous samplings, the prize in their game:
sister to sister . . .

time for my cousins: first she from whose wall
Harlow seductively leers down at all,
then my boy cousin, gray-headed and tall,
buying me ice-cream;

silly tongue-twisting with her, and with him
talk about Franco—prophetic and grim;
then with my uncle: moustachioed, trim,
dunking for apples;

finally past the top landing and out,
bearing home magic, but bumbling about,
seeking my roof door, unable to shout:
"Which is my building?"

lost with the magic so tenderly stewed:
sister to sister embraced through their food . . .
Which is my building??—in panicky mood,
trembling I waken.

5. The Dream Untangled

Trembling I waken—not on a tenement roof
in grassless Brownsville, lost amid ghastly shirts
and sheets and the haggard shrilling of mothers, but safe
beside the balanced breathing of my wife
in my own house: lien-free and termite-free,
as can be proved in notarized reports
filed with the county at the usual fee.

Nor do I clutch a jar of stew; that jar
was rinsed, refilled, and roofward sent—I guess
some forty-seven years ago or more.
And not till three years later did I hear
the lullaby, crooned unaware of me
to that new-hatched, already blighted face
in her benighted room, on her doomed knee,

on some gray street whose name I never allowed
myself to remember, Death Street to my aunt.
And later still the hair of Harlow glowed
in an altogether new, green neighborhood
where one robbed cousin joined my family
while the other, no matter how he felt, was sent
to some mill town where a half-room happened to be.

Of course he wasn't gray-haired then (perhaps
gray-hearted), nor especially tall, although
to me he seemed so; many years, many trips
later, he treated me to one of those cups
of two-cent ices . . . pineapple . . . and we
did talk of Spain, still later—for by now
I went to college and talked knowingly.

The apple-dunking—how did that get in?
Seymour—that uncle—belongs in another dream:
moustachioed, trim . . . such a high-voltage man!
He strung an apple once at Halloween
which sent our jaws on a lunging, biteless spree . . .
At thirty-one, after a handball game,
his heart cracked—no doctor would come—and he

went unflamboyantly into the ground.
As for the building whose roof door I tried
so desperately in my dream to find,
within whose walls so many waltzed and moaned,
not one brick's left of it; I shall not see
either its shape or shade; a sick green sod
is there now; broken jars; rats running free.

6. The Two Uncles

What a mixup of streets, of years, of uncles!
The one who'd have been right for this particular dream
wasn't even home
when in fact I came
with the jar;
he's still alive, sporting eighty-year wrinkles
—not a moustache;
even now his eye Europeanly twinkles:
he's no spender . . . probably hides cash;
never got the hang of a cigar;
never set foot in a bar;
never drove a car—
unlike Uncle Seymour, who one day
during the Depression
—when trainride nickels were rare
and beat-up shoes in fashion—
stopped his brand-new Chevrolet
before our stoop,
causing the neighborhood to gape
in open shock
as haughtily we whizzed away
around the block.

7. *Setting Out Alone*

I sit up sharply; hand under chin,
I struggle out of sleep.
What has aroused my spectral kin
to most
incongruous motion? But of course! it was our noontime trip
past Pennsylvania Avenue, Bay Parkway and the rest,
precious enclaves populous with ghost . . .
Of course! This is how ghosts reply
deep in the night, when one has galloped by
at pre-noon, scarcely noticing the past
out of the corner of his eye.

Wide awake,
determined not to be tracked down
by phantoms I myself should seek—
a Verrazzano, an inspired Drake
in search of all that I've begun, outgrown and done,
I set out, quaking and alone
although beside me, bone to anklebone,
just as she sat
by day,
hushes my wife, too deep within her dream of a green hat
to guess that I have slipped away.

II

1. Back on the Road

I'm back on the road—this time without traffic,
without *Boccaccio*, without green-sparking needles.
Into the corner of my eye, the unborn
grandchild occasionally rises, with the
blurred but important look of someone waiting
beside a carousel's rotations, as I
ride full force 'round a dream-wild diorama
swifter than can be told of it—first passing
my father patient in the place we gave him
twenty-six Februaries ago (the snowfall
had stopped, a bloody sun leaned out as witness);
now off the Island parkway, vaulted onto
the Belt—merry-go-round without music or stallions—
passing the all-night lamp of two who skoaled us
when last year's phone rang pregnant (she wept, somewhat
for joy at our joy, somewhat for being childless;
he, swollen with a more than nine months' creature)

—that night, awake at the same hour as this, supporting
the same cheek with the same fist, before my
reviewing stand, like an emperor, surveying
widowers, widows, expectant and delivered,
that night I made foolish, most unfair demands on
an embryo without fingernails, with scarcely
a heartbeat . . . .

2. Carousel Riders

It takes no time, no time to round them all,
all my old settlements
so separate then . . . light years apart . . .
now clustering points
on a music-box diorama.
And I strain to remember at which of those points
one night, writhing with time,
I saw an oval platform, innocuously churning,
its cavalry forever charging, never advancing,
with only so many bridles
and a line at the ticket booth:
—after that day, perhaps,
when the palsied beldame of invented lips
and the fresh-breasted bank clerk who patronized her
leaned as one toward the window-grating?
when a boy, trying manhood on, brought grandpa by
and lifted him, lowered him into a barber-chair?
when November exposed
three grandmotherly trees
broken amid their straight-backed sprouts?
—or maybe when parents of friends began dying,
when my own father died
soon after his granddaughter's birth . . .

And suddenly I behold *her* unborn child
not as my solace, a delicious elbow
replacing vanished friends,
but as my replacement
on the coldly rising and sinking stallion
I have come after fifty-one years
to consider mine.

3. Bay Parkway

What I would like now
is to go not one yard further on this road.
What I would like
is for a helicopter to lift me
or a ferry to take me on
and over to Jersey,
or a way to zigzag through strange inland streets
till I reach the Verrazzano's, the fire-drake's ramp.

And it is not so much
because one can almost see from the highway
the bedroom on Bay 29th
where my father, through his oxygen tent,
introduced me and the doctor to each other
with one last joke: "Poet and Doctor..."
—a take-off on the overture of Von Suppè.

It is more
because one can almost see the windows
of the basement on Bay 32nd
where, stuffed with caresses and cake, I beheld
the *kazatske* weddings of my six big cousins
(now all widowed or dead).

It is mostly
because one can almost see the stoop
near the corner on Bay 34th
where on a game night in May
I assured the "Milkman" that I'd
"found thirty-six dancing spiders in my milk"—
and for ten whole minutes held to my words without laughing,
no matter what he asked,
until he made me answer that my mother
was thirty-six dancing spiders.

[61]

But no ferry, no helicopter
comes to the rescue;
nor is there time to sneak off the parkway.
In less than a second
my ancient nest of games and welcomes
approaches, passes, not even noticed by the other riders.

And since it would be not just unseemly, unmanly,
but downright dangerous
to turn one's face, even for that second,
and stretch forth one's arms—
firmly I move toward the Bridge,
the by now really rested fire-drake
impatient to take me on his back and fly.

III

1. Soubise

Because the recipe called for at least three cups
of onion thinly sliced,
I sat myself down (an arm's length from the grapes)
and, getting the hang of it after a while, released
from the past
dozens of phantom dinners we'd prepared, to which our friends
          had come,
dozens we'd come to, which our friends prepared,
the menus blended now, the occasions blurred,
the company, cluster by cluster,
like browning bunches of grapes, name after name,
body by body, heading for disaster,
blighted in unpredictable fashion,
in irresistible sequence of attrition.

And because it was onion I sliced, alone at the table,
I let myself weep without control or shame
for faces long grown undistinguishable
and those about to come,
about to hush some of their hungers
and ours with handclasp, and soubise, and jest:
he with the throat condition not to be discussed,
she with the missing marvelous breast;
and for my wife, too crippled in her fingers
especially before rain
to slice an onion thin.

2. *Phone Call*

I don't believe this dinner or its faces
will be blended
with the rest.
Some time before it ended
—in fact, just as I passed
the casserole and Dave cried, "The soubise is
out of this world!" the telephone
rang out its tidings like a new year's bell:
our daughter's toil was done—
nine yammering pounds had joined us in the noontide sun—
full-faced, full-fingered, and female.

Nora Elizabeth! *her* graduations!
her first daughter!
—From this night
I'll drink less wine, more water,
cross only at the light,
go off on longer, frequenter vacations,
do twenty push-ups twice a day,
seize the slick reins of my uncaring roan
and make the beast obey
for one more up and down before he's done with me
and takes my great-granddaughter on.

Indeed, I'll be back on the Belt tomorrow,
pass my old
entrances,
old exit signs, behold
through a new pair of eyes
new birds, new baseball diamonds, a new borough,
the um-pa-pa of Von Suppè
outshouted as I pass my father's aisle
with hurrying hurray
away via fire-drake across the Lower Bay
perhaps to answer her first smile.

TWO VISITS

This was the weekend of two visits:
yesterday a long drive to short minutes,
convinced that my first grandchild
(in my arms for the first time) smiled
not because of gas
but at a fingering caress,
that her eye acknowledged my possessive gaze,
her ear my nonsense-praise,
that every involuntary spasm of her foot and fist
proclaimed an Olympic free-style medalist.

This was the weekend of two visits:
today a short drive to long minutes,
convinced that my father's yew
(unshorn for some time) knew
who leaned with shears
to trim the wildness of three years,
that like a lonesome hand it sought my hand,
its touch a reprimand,
that his brother tombstones all along the row
prepared to upbraid me as soon as I should go.

This was the weekend of two visits
whose order did not lift my spirits.
For them, on the other hand,
it could not have been better planned:
to him I brought her
smile—medalist great-granddaughter!
to her I brought his touch, his voice, his wish—
heirlooms rare and fresh
kept warm through twenty-seven winters; not the blight
that otherwise might chill her crib tonight.

II
Zudioska

THE REDWING'S CRY

Sharp and silver
and mislaid these forty years
suddenly through my ears
comes the redwing's cry,
turns the lock
that held back the river;
it is six o'clock
and I . . .

I do not stop to wonder whether I am in the valley
or the valley is in me.
Dew soaks my sneakers.
Everywhere a scent of rising, opening creatures
halloos me and my heart trumpets.
Longer than widest armspread can encompass
flows the river toward mysterious turnings
past Cornwall in the south and in the north the burning
windows of Newburgh; but whatever lies
within the compass of arms, of eyes,
is mine today, mine forever,
the river in me, I in the river.

A long time I lie still,
as if the roar of hair against pillow
will ruin the redwing's work, return the terror
of rising to meet a mirror . . .

till I'm uncertain
whether I heard
an actual bird
or a fiction,
and, if real,
whether it will sound again;
whether it came as ordeal
or benediction.

GRANDDAUGHTER ON BEACH

1.

That apricot protuberance of belly and buttock
against the gnash of breaker, the blanch of shell,
is less nutritious than seditious—like those tomatoes
in Hitler Paris hurling the Internationale from Picasso's sill.

2.

The sea's big guns begin; its offensive reaches her toes;
I scoop her up; we escape over Maginot shellbits lining the sand
as, foetal-safe, under my arm she curls, and through three layers of
        clothes
fixes her gulf-cold imprint as surely as a great rancher's brand.

PHONE CALL

Dry, remote
as the Long Island leaf
my granddaughter
this morning set afloat
from shallow water
toward the open seas,
I phone
Los Angeles
where, more than half my life,
Mother's
been heaped with singing
friends unknown
to me. It's ringing.
We rejoice
at the good health in one another's
voice.
What more? Talked out?

No; she reminds herself
to ask about
that sparkling elf
and thank me for the photograph
(it sits already on her shelf).
Then I report with what a victory laugh
the infant watched her leaf become a boat.
At this, across three thousand miles of wire, across
eighty-one years, without
the loss
of half a decibel, half
a hemidemisemiquaver note,
the absolutely identical laughter of my mother
leaps
at one parched hand,
while the other
frantically grips
the morning outcry of my grand-
daughter, who, amid heaps
of plastic friends
unknown to me, on a New Jersey pillow sleeps,
only a smile now nudging at those lips
as in a dream
she sends
her arboretum leaf once more downstream
toward the great ships.

VISITING HOUR: At the Swanholm, St. Petersburg

Despising the driveway's allure, the tree-guised
parking-lot, the spruces' fraudulent greening,
the front door's hail, bright as a tart's lips—
one says the stark;

one says there is no afterlife, no guerdon
for the good, no fire for the fiendish, all
are only inventions to keep the outrageous
in check—and you agree;

one says no human weave, not even
the most colossal, is sturdier than a spider's,
connecting ever fewer, held finally by one,
then none—and you agree;

and you agree that nothing of crowning importance,
nothing that either proves or questions
is likely to be done or said in one of these
nursing homes

where, even if you looked quite hard at the faces pinned
to a pillow or drooped forward in a wheelchair,
you couldn't readily notice there'd been substitutions
since last night;

and you agree that the odds are against its being
worth the effort to lean encouragingly
toward her whose singing white strands of autumn
now sit shorn

so that she's a triplet between shorn neighbors,
a rough-smocked, expressionless threesome who, never daring
to ring for the brash attendant, surrender at last
to wetting themselves;

she will probably, in an hour, have forgotten that it was
you who bothered to visit, that the flowers
are hers; and . . . you see . . . she cannot even decide
what year she was born . . .

or can she? . . . Yes! it was '89—she's certain!
her mumbling begins to be easier to decode:
she's a girl in Russia, with clothes so ragged,
it keeps her from school;

and mother sends her across the fields to grandpa,
who's quite well-off, and quite well-known for his books:
Show him your rags, say you need clothing-
money for school . . .
and he, the pious, the prosperous, praised by all
the village, he for whose soul no Kaddish
has sounded in fifty years, whose well-gnawed gravemark
Hitler trod,

suddenly bursts from between his grandchild's bloodless
lips, entering you: *Take a*
potato sack, and cut your legs two holes,
and go to school!

A WEDDING IN LOS ANGELES

On Sunday at 2 P.M. in the Temple Akiba
the hands of the organist strike; then down the aisle
exactly as at the rehearsal, but now in costume,
they march, eyes forward, aware of us twisting sideways
to witness the strewing of flowers, the grandmothers' stride,
the balance of bridesmaid and usher, aware as well
of the crouched photographer careful to catch their motion.

On Sunday at 2:15 in the Temple Akiba
before the rabbi, under the canopy, perches
a pair of tremulous doves, aware of us straining
to witness the Word he rains on their awe, the word
they'd written each other in contract, the word they scarcely
have breath to repeat when commanded, aware as well
of the crouched photographer careful to catch their moment.

On Sunday at 3 P.M. in the banqueting-hall
of the Temple Akiba a hundred and fifty guests,
boisterous now, having witnessed that which they witnessed,
move with a clasping of hands, an embracing, a praising,
first to their food, then to the *sher*, the *freilachs*,
the *hora*, treading all griefs underfoot, aware
of the crouched photographer careful to catch their joyance.

On Sunday at 4:25, outdoors for a draught
of air, one notices traffic thundering down
Sepulveda Boulevard, slowing not in the least
before the Temple Akiba, as if unaware
that the band is now playing a waltz, the bride now whirls
with her father, the groom with his mother, carefully caught
for all time by the crouched photographer.

QUEBEC

By now it is really late.
Our backs face one another.
My left hand finds her right
for the gentle mutual pressure.

Suddenly I recall
that the bed in which we are lying
is a few minutes' walk from the wall
through which Montcalm came dying.

And only a few miles off
a landscape seemingly peaceful
still writhes at the drum and fife
proclaiming Wolfe successful.

On streets entranced by their truce,
whose dream we so admire,
there could be no excuse
to break our own cease-fire.

For my sake she denied
several bright windows;
for hers, I disobeyed
several gray windings.

Yet, like two locked foes,
we fought our fight as always:
poetry versus prose,
on hilltops, in hallways.

Twice on the battle-line
there came to me a question:
will I ever be back alone
to wrap myself in this bastion?

But between the pressure of hand
in hand and the fall into dreaming,
I am answered; I understand;
nothing will come of my scheming.

No, I will never be back
alone on the St. Lawrence
to wring from the stones of Quebec
whatever may be their substance.

In through the siege-proof wall
my death would seep to find me;
unto my death all
these ancient windings would wind me.

On my Plains of Abraham,
whether in room or alley,
like my brothers Wolfe and Montcalm
I would fell and be felled in the volley.

She sleeps. No need to tell
why I press her hand as tightly
as were she the Citadel
that guards this city nightly.

VICTORIA STATION

Gatwick at two A.M. lay so forsaken;
a train pulled in; we thought it best to go.
All the way to Victoria a Jamaican
raved about London, especially Mme. Tussaud:
"You fear that at your touch the wax will waken!"
But came Victoria, her clammy glow
told us at once our hope had been mistaken:
here was no life, but a gray-blue tableau.

The Grosvenor Hotel, in mournful neon,
soliloquized on its more gorgeous youth.
Two yellow clocks had managed to agree on
a joint communique, a common truth:
"It's forty-three past two!" With Ponce de Leon
absent, the Bar gleamed like a last gold tooth.
None of those waiting wished his looks to be on
such prints as proffered by the Photo Booth;

none—not the creature, drowsing or fordrunken,
curled in midstation on a ledge; the pair
entwined in lust or weariness, deep sunk in
an alcove's shade; the crone crouched as in prayer
for life, or a locker to leave her wretched trunk in;
nailed uncomplaining to a bench, arms bare,
the frost- or palsy-mastered girl; half shrunken
nearby, the fellow with a sad affair

where nose and chin should be—burnt or a leper—
who turned revulsion into a career
by vending bits of turquoise-festering paper
at five pence each; the luggage folk, with fear
or longing sculpted faces, London's caper
or nightmare finished or to come, now here
museumed in Victoria's pre-dawn vapor
no matter how they did or may appear

on other days, now here, no animation
of limb or lip. Suddenly, from far tracks,
a rush of wheels; ears wake; but the vibration
rings hollow: four carts, tumbrils heaped with sacks,
are ferried vulgarly across the station.
Though on the Board nor time nor destination
is legible, enough illumination
falls on the bench, toward which, in widening arcs,
forever supervised by those two clocks,
the tumbrils roll, atrocious transportation,
heaped high, it seems in that half-light, with packs
of mail, or persons yellowing into wax.

[75]

WESTMINSTER SYNAGOGUE

Ears afire, I knock at Kent House door.
My hands could not protect them if I tried
except from the drone of Heathrow jets, the roar
of a bus marked "Kensington." Too deep inside,
the tick of an Irish bomb at Harrod's store,
the swords forever committing chivalricide
athwart Knightsbridge, the million-footed squall
from Victoria's trains to Exhibition Hall.

The door shuts out those ghosts storming the Park
across the way; the dignity and calm
of my friend Rabbi uncurtaining his Ark
halts the old swords, defuses the young bomb.
But smilingly he chooses to remark
that where the Torah blazes now, Madame
de St. Laurent enjoyed her fireplace,
herself enjoyed through long years by His Grace

the Duke of Kent. At once his royal groans
roll 'round the room, her murmured syllables
mock what the cantor loftily intones.
But now a door is opened; silence drills
my skull; it fills my rib-cage, chills my bones.
With dignity, with calm the Rabbi tells
that in this room heal fifteen hundred holy
scrolls a scribe has been repairing slowly,

and as each wraith-loved Torah is repaired,
some living congregation takes it in.
—Not for such future were these writings spared,
the Rabbi makes me understand: Berlin
had a museum in mind; these would be aired
as trophies of a tribe that once had been.
I ask: Might one be opened?—but at once
desist . . . No need! Madame de St. Laurent's

syllables, and the groans of her high lover,
are hammered into dust by the dear notes
that—scroll by scroll, rack under rack—recover
their Sabbath force. Seventy thousand throats
flame in my ears. The interview is over;
I'm at the bus stop; but around me floats
a choral fire from every synagogue
of Brno, Pilsen, Bratislava, Prague.

GILBERT AND SULLIVAN NIGHT AT THE
PROMS

Of course, it included the women's section, gaudily
gowned, seated now motionless, still hearing
(despite an intermission) spectacular
passages of their hymn to Princess Ida;
but that wasn't it; nor was it the males in somber
attire, straining like cocks now to declare
that they indeed, definitively *are*
gentlemen of Japan; nor the soloists
grinning into the pit where growths of hair
bobbed up and down, straw hats came off and on,
Union Jacks and balloons took attitudes
suitably "queer and quaint"; of course, it included
all that, but that wasn't it; nor was it just
the being in Albert Hall, the acoustical bigness,
the adoring hush, tier upon tier, of twenty
thousand, sucking eighth-notes like hard candy,
though certainly it included that; nor was it
the seventy-year-old organist from Ipswich
whose son was to meet her midnight train, who'd helped
defend her airdrome from the claw of Hitler,
who was born, along with thirteen brothers and sisters,
in a thatched house they couldn't afford to buy,

who remembers rising at 5 A.M. to help
her mother bake bread in an old brick oven,
whose mother ("the finest woman I ever knew")
lived to a hundred and three, who didn't know
why she was telling us these things—though surely
that too was part of it; but it was mostly
another perfect night, five years before,
when Romeo leaped and Juliet whirled away
their childhood and all eyes in Covent Garden
caressed their fragile ecstasy. Even then
I had known it included more, included the fragile
ecstasy repeated in all eyes,
that instant when I'd gathered in the whole
audience, like a grandfather observing
cherubic skaters on a lake who laugh
as if the blood will never turn to ice,
as if the ice will never turn to blood.

GRANDPARENTS IN LONDON

We are aging,
gripped
by bitterness, by doubt.
My camera sets her raging.
When asked to comment on her hair,
I blurt out:
"Nondescript."
And we're beginning to forget
when we were where.
By Tuesday both are in a fret
as to which restaurant
we tried
following the Sunday sail to Greenwich.

If after two nights' sleep we can't
remember on which side
of Thames we supped, how shall we manage
to separate this London stay
from any other?
Shall we say
it was the time
we started to display
the typical deportment
of grandfather-and-mother,
plucking from Oxford Street a prime
assortment
of rattles, books, and dolls?
Shall we say it was the time we gaped not at St. Paul's
but at Paul Scofield; not at Parliament but the Proms;
hosted not by Carlyle and Dickens in their houses
but by once-gracious monarchs and their spouses
at Windsor?—two finally fiftyish Americans
nearly found by Irish bombs
at Euston Station,
nearly lost by meeting plans
that never went awrier: she
joyless at Keats' House, expecting me,
I in the lobby of the Tate,
from 3:15 to 4,
afraid to quit the door—
wild with the long wait
for public phones,
messages no one would deliver,
imagined moans,
imagined leaps into the river—
finally, frantic with waiting,
hating
the stupid camera still in my grip
whose click, throughout the trip,

from Haymarket to Hampton Court to Bath,
had roused her wrath,
ready now to smash to smithereens
the lens that had focused on so many scenes,
now focusing on, imagining everywhere
as the cab rocketed from Square to Square
one subject only, one half-gray head of hair.

LOCATION

"How was the hotel?"
One grew accustomed to St. Pancras' bell
at the left eardrum every quarter hour;
the narrow tub turning one's shower
into a hero's test;
the cold, limp breakfast toast;
the bankrupt bathroom light;
the clock
that had apparently gone into shock
one morning or one night
at five past seven;
and at the register the white-haired female raven.

What one never grew
nor ever shall grow quite accustomed to
were (just across the lane) a pair of dates
marking the residence of Yeats;
and halfway down the street
a sacramental plate
from Abrahamic times
plus more
in that museum on the second floor;
and next to Pancras' chimes
a stop for buses
to Shakespeare's crones, and Chaucer's bones, and the king's
crosses.

JOURNAL ENTRY

After savoring for years, lavishing praise
for years, on two exotic days
of sex and slaughter, finally
we were to lean
once more spellbound from Old Bailey's balcony.

Waked at six-fifteen,
we threw some clothes on, downed
some breakfast, drilled through the underground
to St. Paul's Station, shot
startlingly forward, and at nine-
fifty secured our spot
seventh on line.

At last, as if he'd heard
my wife's poor kneecaps shrieking
in the damp, a guard appeared and started speaking;
but his was not the gentle word
of four years back. "No cameras allowed!"
he lashed the crowd
—as if expecting a salute—
and pertly brushed from his official suit
my cry: "Unfair!
You should at least provide
a place somewhere
to leave one's camera!"—Meanwhile
(and who could blame them?) with a smile
those back of us, having had time to hide
their Kodaks, moved ahead in double file
to take the seats we pioneers
had been denied.

Chagrined,
faces burning to the ears,
we stood a long time in the morning wind
and let the city map
ridiculously flap

[81]

before we found that we could lift our feet,
though heavily, and got on the wrong bus,
and off at the next stop, and no one seemed to know
except one lady, sweet
in the old London way, who misdirected us
nearly a mile past Chancery Row.

We licked our wounds on an old bench near Lincoln's Inn.
Recalling our first stroll along Fleet Street
a score of years ago,
how poor we'd been,
too poor to eat
even the cheapest listing at the Cheshire Cheese
(although her unarthritic knees
could climb to the top landing in one-third
the time), and how today whatever dish might please
our fancy we could have with ease,
it occurred
to both at once, that we were most
likely to forget Old Bailey
by lunching where Sam Johnson, Goldsmith, and the rest
had gathered daily,
and where
perhaps a ghost
of laughter following a jest
might still enrich the air.

If such indeed were there,
it must have hidden from the plush
Atlanta person and his plusher guest
whose table, in that noon-hour crush,
we had to share.
As for the luncheon fare,
it bore no more relation
to its price
than did our partners' tasteless conversation
to Samuel Johnson's spice.

Across the yard, at Johnson's door, two women
almost old enough to have let him in
after his outings, did the same
for me. I had the poor taste to exclaim
how crowded were
these chambers twenty years
before.
"Johnson's not on examinations any more,"
said one in tears.
How could I comfort her,
I, their only customer,
but buy up every postcard in the place?

Across the river, on the promenade,
too early for ther matinee,
as if some god
had chosen us to preview a new play
at which no tickets were required
and had hired
an actor on his lunchtime break,
we watched an actual thespian take
his kite to the Thames railing, try
to make its peacock spirit fly,
and having raised it not one inch
nearer the sky,
give up at last and leave us on our bench
not knowing whether the kite stood for his heart,
not knowing whether we were meant to cry
or laugh, not knowing whether to applaud his art.

The indoors play, the one
for which we'd paid,
was more professionally done:
no question what it stood for—
three beds, four couples, a charade,
exactly what we needed, good for
an afternoon of laughter.

Fifteen minutes after,
the bus outspat us with the rest
at Piccadilly; pornographic
establishments had got the best
of less audacious traffic;
parents in vain pulled sons away
from an array
of neon hip and breast,
some arranged in Sapphic
postures,
unmistakable their look, their gestures.

We, with our final strength, managed to find
a vaunted seafood place, and there we dined.
Perhaps by then it was a case of mind
over—a perfectly acceptable
crab-salad, which unfortunately tasted like a fresh-dyed wool.

The couple next to us had ordered
something seasoned with Marsala wine.
Their rapture was beyond belief; in fact, it bordered
on the asinine.
Every second word: "Marsala!"—reverend
as the refrain of an old hymn—
they warbled to the waiter,
trumpeted "Marsala!" to a late-arriving friend.
In a crab-salad trance I made them swim
miles of Marsala red...

        We strolled
through Aldwych, somewhat early for the play.
Next to the theatre a tablet told
that here Novello dwelt.
Unlike our young Marsala pair
(whose hearts leap up when they behold
anything anywhere)
I felt

nothing. Nor did I go insane
between two vintage Ibsen acts
at finding myself poised to drink a gin
and tonic over Drury Lane.

Considering the facts,
our banishment from Old Bailey may have been
a blessing . . . Happier about
Ibsen than the world
he slashed at, back to our hotel we swirled,
having miraculously succeeded
in clawing onto a bus without
being stampeded,
and won, for seven pence
apiece,
beside the ride,
almost as much suspense
as Ibsen's audience
—including promises of homicide
from two young punks who tried
to travel free, until police
stepped forward and recited London's laws
like twin Poloniuses aching for applause.

Acts
were what we wanted. All the world's a stage,
and we had tickets!—Oh, we'd got
the *Times*, but for the entertainment page,
not
for that day's facts.

Toward our hotel we noticed at the Cora,
the Tavistock, the New Ambassador, a
parade of taxis out of which
tumbled the rich,
about to lend a dullish register
their aura.

[85]

The seductive stir
of window curtains on an upper floor
shot through me; lamplight underneath a door
ignited me;
and from another, slightly
open, burst
lips, tongues, fingers lightly
quenching each other's thirst—
while on behalf of B.B.C.
a tenor brightly
addressed them,
blessed them,
incited and expressed them:
You're my day; you're my night—
when you're beside me, it's all right.

Turning the key, at last
we're locked inside.
Teeth are brushed.
Passion gathers and goes past.
The radio has died;
there'll be
no further entertainment
until Old Bailey's first arraignment
tomorrow. Somewhere a toilet's flushed;
it has the ring of truth; it comes at me
like a particularly vicious item on page three
that, without warning,
struck this morning,
just in time to spoil it,
as I was squeezing lemon in my tea.

The flushing of a stranger's toilet
never fails to give me cramps
and make me philosophic
—a fearful state at best, but catastrophic
when, with the purest of intentions,
my wife turns off the lamps.

Suddenly London sprawls
before me all its grand dimensions:
swarms on Oxford, gems
of sunlight on the Thames,
remain; St. Paul's
astride its skyline, Nelson astride his Square,
speakers astride their
Corner, double-decker buses everywhere
remain; no matter if the Empire falls,
this room, this bed remain
to entertain
another pair
while we, our three weeks ended, glare
again
at the grim door
behind which, like a wolf out of his wits
with hunger, sits
a three weeks' growth of gloom
ready to leap
with a devouring roar
at us, and at those lovers in a nearby room
the B.B.C. seems to have lulled asleep:
Shut the window on the night;
everything will be all right.

LAST NIGHT IN BRUSSELS

Not saucily, like Brussels' mannikin,
eternally bright Flanders, for whom years
are nothing, at my midnight font again
I stand, over the Boulevard Jacqmain.

Our last night bawls away on a loud collision
of cobblestone and beer-truck; into my ears
blunders a drunken song that wakes a vision
of blotched eyes ripe for Boschian derision.

I envy the drenched blindness of such singers,
for neither Belgium's quaintness nor her beers
have quenched this crazy thirst of mine which lingers
despite all guzzling. Flanders flows through my fingers.

I'd hoped that, with one hour of concentration,
the Groote Markt would rock once more with cheers
as ghost by ghost old Bruges' population
roused to some ceremonious occasion.

Instead I hear behind Tournai's Te Deums
Huguenot shrieks, and under the veneers
of haughty colleges lurk mausoleums,
and in the galleries of great museums

Rubens shows Pilate smirking from the castles
of Flanders at the sight of Antwerp spears
plunged in the side of Christ—Van Eyck's apostles
rush hounded up the alleyways of Brussels.

So, finished, of this boulevard accursed
I beg forgiveness, though nobody hears—
despite much drinking, drier than at first;
clutching at Flanders with my crazy thirst.

VIEW OF DELFT

Circling Vermeer's Delft, I asked
our sailor—an ingratiating, enterprising lad—
whether the neo-classic structure overhead
with Hebrew letters poorly masked
was once a synagogue. His smile grew faint,
then vanished altogether: "Yes,"
anticipating my next guess,
"the Germans." "Can a town permit one coat
of Nazi paint
to erase
five centuries of ghosts?" His face
grew honest. "You
have come to Europe and aboard my boat
to find what's old.
Our Delft is new; we're new;
we're tired of being told
ghost tales, no matter how tremendous or how true."
At this he turned his back
on my gray hairs and questions. An exotic doll
with eyes and tresses black
as any ever mirrored in a Dutch canal
engaged him; each had read the other's sign;
that night, if all went well,
he'd share at least her wine
while, like a coat of paint, a seeping in of gas,
    the dusk engulfed
—gable by gable—Vermeer's Delft.

THE LAST SUPPER

Who but Leonardo could conjure me onto his wall,
choosing, of all traumatic moments, my very worst?

Years he wrought, till even he was satisfied
it really was I who sat there
central amid the apostles, tranquil-faced
while storming them with my charge of betrayal.
It seemed the Master had worked with hammer, not brush,
nailing me there, dooming me
ever to hold the aspect of calm
though never again in this life would I sup.

But backed by plaster and paste
my tempera being took hope.
By 1517 (thanks to Milan's humidity)
I felt myself peeling free.
By Borromeo's time I was so far gone,
the Cardinal ordered a copy made;
and when Torre in 1674 sighed "Lost!"
I, half-reascended already,
could hardly restrain my lips from an alleluia.

Then it began: two centuries of crucifixion
sans tree, hill, or nails:
restorations, alterations
limply pinning me down to the plaster—a me
ravaged and scarcely me;
till at last, at last, in August, 1943
(as the German guide tells it, without identifying the planes)
"wurde das Refektorium
durch Bombenwurf schwer beschädigt
und blieb ohne Dach und Fenster."

Cursed be the miracle that spared me
as I was positioning for ascension!
Three walls gone, and the roof,
while we, unbudged, kept at the wine and meat!
What use to pray
that in rain and heat
I would at last go loose?
Just as from the start I could have guessed
Judas' deal and all the rest,
I knew my "friends" would soon be back
busy with new techniques,
putting the refectory together again,
strengthening my entrapment,
with a Mauro Pelliccioli in the end
to lift the botchwork
from my agonized tranquility.

—Thus move the pale lips of the Christ.
But his story takes too long.
As he gauges the agitation of his followers,
a Japanese couple peer at a map of the city, arguing,
coldly a Frenchman takes flash pictures,
a Swede, unasked, explains the "composition" to his wife,
a victorious Italian writes down a girl's address,
and I, desperate for a stirring of the blood,
stand there, stand there, until it strikes me
that what he has finally resigned himself to
is not so much his passion as his mission:
probing the treacheries of our devotions, paling
year by year in the humidity of Milan
and in the glare of our predatory lens.

PIAZZA DEL CAMPIDOGLIO

1.

Call it our sickness, call it our syndrome.
In every town, the two very buildings
lunged at by tourists, are those we flee.
No longer picturesque do they bend:
a hen, a rooster cuddling their brood—
but like twin vampires straddle the town:
each street, the vein of a throat sucked dry.
My wife gets a chill in every cathedral:
slabs and walls kill the sunlight inside her;
she longs to break loose, to find the shoe-stores.
And in the great halls of converted palazzi
her feet become tired, her eyes become tired;
she must find a bench that faces a wall
on which, for a change, Christ is not nailed.
She goes to please me; I, because one must.
But part of me winces at ghost-congregations
whipped to their knees, the penny torn loose,
the rage swung against sinners, skeptics.
Nor can I gaily stroll across floors
burnished in blood, rejoice at domes
adorned by decree, ignore the hollow
dungeons sounding at every tread,
gasp down the cliffs of castles where witches
used to be dropped, their shriek like a streamer
fluttering after them: "Innocent! Innocent!"
—And so, when saucy, I washed a peach
at the sacred fountain before St. Peter's;
and so, when sensible, I come
unwillingly again to Rome.

2.

Matteotti!
Saint of my boyhood,
champion who alone held back the surge,
whose silence Mussolini craved
as humans crave meat—
in every town, a second Jesus,
you stand now: hallowed and raped:
Piazza di Matteotti,
via di Matteotti . . .
But while the old debate elections in Bologna's Square,
"FUAN!" bray the university walls;
through Milan the handbills fly:
"Enough disorder!
It is time for the police!"
Across the Strait *Tribuna* screams:
"*Caos in Sicilia!*
Siamo la Merce degli Agitatori Sindacali!"
The flags of Palermo are at half-staff
—not for Palermo, but against Biafra.
In Naples, not far from the U.S. naval base,
"*Viva Il Re!!*" streams bold from boulevard windows,
and the man at the railroad
displays Il Duce verses
inscribed on ceramic tiles.
A gang of fledgling assassins in Rome,
noticing "Dany the Red" at a table,
drag him away from his friends and beat him
in the Piazza di Colonna
while people and police stand by,
while passengers in trams
lip a newspaper headline:
"Who killed Marlene in the Villa Borghese?"
Matteotti!
What a speech you would deliver now
if I could lift from your mouth
the soil of forty-five years!

[93]

3.

Overnight the golden name is plastered
on every wall in Rome:
Commemorazione!
Wednesday the 10th of June . . .
Alla Memoria di Giacomo Matteotti
Ucciso dalla Barbarie Fascista
Per Difendere gli Ideali del Socialismo . . .
Tell it! Tell it!
In case the old have forgotten,
in case the young don't know,
tell how it happened in 1924,
how they struck him down for Il Duce,
how Il Duce, denying the murder that gave his intestines joy,
silenced, through Giacomo's silence,
all Italy . . .
for twenty polluted years.

Ah, suddenly in the snow of Matteotti posters
Rome has grown bearable.
To the Capitol, to the Capitol
let us go!
At the Piazza del Campidoglio
let us assemble!
In thousands, hundred thousands,
let us avenge
by our roar
past Jupiter's ghost eternally deaf in his ghost temple
avenge by our roar
unto the dusking sky
not only the saint of my boyhood, Matteotti,
but Peter, Cecilia, and all the rest
martyred for being new,
gallowed, broiled, sliced, hurled innocent
down the Tarpeian Rock,
thrust amid lions across the way there
while Marcus Aurelius waved to the crowd.

Wafted on Judgment's wind
I ascend Michelangelo's stairs
scarcely seeing or touching them,
pinning the rosette on my lapel
clumsily, because my eyes are full.

4.

Half empty the Square. Half empty
the glare of the sun, which once
was Apollo; there, on the dais
(it is a state affair, after all),
alongside the featured pair whose phrase
half empty drifts through the air,
two rigidly stationed officers
wear white helmets (half empty)
and seem to share the emperor Marcus'
half empty stare astride his stallion
without a care for Giacomo's name
which the loudspeakers
blare to several hundred
of middle-aged hair. Half empty
vows. Half empty the Square.

5.

Noting his gentle aspect
on the day they lifted horse and king
from Tiber's bed
after seven centuries sunk in clay,
one, marveling, turned to the rest
and said: "Victory
must have driven the Goth insane; why else
would he have drowned a face
so mild?" —Accursed face,
that (as each rose of pain
burst from the Colisseum) sweetly smiled!

were I the conqueror now, I too
would take that face
from its high station;
for the sake of mobbed Rienzi,
Matteotti slaughtered,
back into Tiber's bed
it should be cast, to moulder
till those eyes
for once have watered, and from that bronze mouth
rots the smile at last!

6.

Those few who climbed, who might have been at dinner,
wait as though for a word that will set them aflame
if any word can, or (while the Transport Minister
drones on: *"In nomen di Matteotti . . ."*)
seek out acquaintances, or mildly gaze at the hecklers
—new Matteottis, perhaps, at whom the police in their cars
glare, greedy for silence, dreaming
to drag each by the scruff of the neck, young zealot,
and fling him
in the good old way
from Tarpe rock.

It was then I fled to the edge of the hill,
just over the Forum,
and swept my sight around Rome,
seeking the quarter
in which Matteotti's assassins, old men now
(who footloose prowled for twenty years while earth
hardened above his lips),
old men now, old grinning men
with married grandchildren,
enjoy the antipasto of their house arrest.

And once more Titus Andronicus
bellows from below for Justice;
once more, unanswered by this hill of hills,
turns his appeal from Jupiter to Pluto.
Oh, were I saucy, I would be pulling
my wife down Michelangelo's stairs
—three at a time!
mocking the hope with which I climbed—
with Titus bellowing: *"Dost thou perceive
that Rome is but a wilderness of tigers?"*
and—glad the city wall is broken—
flee, by the first express, to Genoa!
But being sensible, I quietly say: "Come!"
let her convince me to unpin the rosette
as down the stairs we slowly back away
toward streets which have no other care
than being streets and finding out
who killed Marlene in the Villa Borghese.

SUNDAY IN THE SQUARE: San Miguel de Allende

Arm half-raised, about to summon from their stumbling
knees, their crumbling stalls, their grumbling countrysides
the great-great-great-grandchildren of his Revolution,
astride his steed Allende rides.

Circling him slower than the hand of a gigantic
clock, an ancient man who does not openly beg
hobbles by; gripped by its best remaining bristles,
an ancient broom is his third leg.

A dried-out woman bending to the dried-out pavement
keeps arranging, rearranging her fourteen
dried-out avocados, facing toward the sunlight
those which are still a little green.

A blind man, not yet twenty-five but pulseless, drowses
too far forward into noon; the deep tin cup
spurts from his fingers; through gray lips a thankyou barely
crawls for the two coins gathered up.

And though Allende's stallion strains, it's no more likely
than the five-peso one a lad struggles to pry
from its onyx base, to break loose and fly forward
with the old enflaming cry.

AT FOUR MINUTES TO ONE

It is four minutes to one.
As the tourbus makes its final turn,
San Miguel suddenly rolls out before them
its quaint adobe streets and graceful domes
—a sight to remember, they decide—
and the clocktower tells them
it is four to one.

Four to one.
A plain old Indian
enters on her knees the plain old church of la Salud
and on her knees approaches the poor altar
as an aged man
with back irreparably warped
fumbles in his rags for a coin,
drops it in the wooden box,
and hobbles forth
mumbling a faint appeal.

At four to one
on the main square, the Jardin,
a huge man from Texas
buys up loud bouquets
at which his señorita, smiling, scolds

[98]

and he orders them
the most expensive lunch
while squatting at the gutter
inert except for hand and mouth
a shawled squaw draws chunks of moldy bread
from her miserable bundle
and stuffs them through her jaws
as if to gag a scream.

At four to one a makeshift bus,
not riveted but stapled,
provided not with windows
but with toy saints
and *Perdóneme, Dios!* scrawled (just in case)
above the driver's wheel,
prepares (unlike Allende timeless on horseback near the bus stop)
to set out
with fourteen drab-eyed, gaudy-fabricked Mexicans
for mysterious drudgeries
amid the monster cacti two miles out of town
and a Manhasset couple
on their way to a private locker room with Roman tub
beside the healing waters, the hotel.

At four to one,
far from the tourist office, the bookstore, the malteds,
against an egregiously rotting wall
which this claptrap bus is about to pass,
three rotting dogs
put spiritlessly each his nose,
then each a lifted leg
while in the shallow end of a long pool
soon to be stepped into by the Manhasset couple
five chubby corporation children from Mexico City,
each with five names,
coaxed by grandmama for one more swim before *comida*,

join hands, led by their governess'
professional smile,
in a photogenic ring-around-the-rosy.

And at four to one, a Norte Americano
about to join the bus for Guanajuato,
the first-class bus with stuck toilet door,
the bus now making its final turn,
buys up every copy of that picturesque card
showing San Miguel
precisely as the passengers see it—
adobe streets and graceful domes—
precisely as he has decided to remember it after one day's
               "research"
while a student from St. Louis,
just seventeen today,
whose first pot—imperfect but unique—of Mexican clay
will be drying soon on a rack at the Instituto,
whose apprentice rug—of Mexican lambhair—
is about to begin its slow blue song on a Belles Artes loom,
voyages her soul
away from the traffic policeman,
the long-distance phone booth,
the Banco Commercial,
down its first side-street
slipping at times on the rain-slick stones
that have not quite washed away the dog-droppings,
frightened less each time she slips,
each time a sombrero's shadow touches her,
adding San Miguel to her soul, cobble by cobble,
adding her soul to San Miguel, cobble by cobble,
finding at last, near the fourth crossing,
her true birthday gift—
not the tin mirror in the store-front,
though she may buy it,
but her own searching eyes
reflected in the pane.

DOGS OF SAN MIGUEL

By night, by day, though next to hopeless
you force your buckling legs
down the exhausted ways of San Miguel,
led on by clues left against walls
by despondent cousins
like messages of explorers vanishing in the Antarctic.

Inspired by despair, your teeth wrestle from the stones
whatever human noses have missed
or fingers been too feeble to displace,
and for a long moment,
chewing what perhaps contains your death,
you lift your heads as if in triumph,
pretending to yourselves that what you have is food.

Facing away from one another,
you couple at high noon right in the Sunday market
unabashed either by first-class Yankee tourists
or by fifth-class buses heading for near towns
—ensuring a new mongrel agony next year;
otherwise you get out of the way at once
when anyone passes, even a small child,
as if grown wise after kicks and rocks enough,
as if afraid of offending for the space you occupy.

How many of you are there now, this day, without collars?
Do you keep statistics?
Can you wonder why seventeen sunrises have passed
since you sniffed a particular urine?
Have rumors reached you concerning poison campaigns
against the collarless?
Could one of you comprehend and translate for others
what the white lady said
in your presence, coolly, in English,
about trucks soon coming by
with gentler, discreeter, more total solutions?
Do you worry?

[101]

Or is there within you by now,
side by side with your zest for every new sun,
a surrender, a prayer
that the next cob of corn you attack
will be poisoned,
the next truck that quietly pulls up beside you
will waft you away with your cousins
to Auschwitz, if not to Nirvana?

Some of you seem to have awaited us.
You watch us approach on our way home from the singing tavern
as if midway down that desolate midnight lane
was our appointed rendezvous,
and you join us on the final lap
halting when we halt,
taking far-fetched encouragement
in our not shooing you off,
fantasizing that we will at last be the ones
to recognize in you the dog of our life
—until the great hacienda doors
half open to let us in
and we succeed in not looking back to meet your eyes
as the doors shut.

But what about you—you three—
three of differing shapes, colors, sizes,
perched like lookouts on the roof of the corner shoppe:
were you hired to guard the fifty-peso ornaments at night,
or is this where you have climbed to take your final stand
after all the rest are wiped out
—like the boys of Chapultepec,
like the warriors atop the last flaming tower of Warsaw's ghetto?

Sometimes I imagine that you are preparing
to howl forth a galvanizing alarm
which we two-legged ones will not at first understand
but at which every last remnant of your legions

will lift his head
and emerge from the shadows:
>Enough sniveling! enough self-loathing!
>enough thanks for being cursed instead of kicked!
>enough willingness to stay asleep
>with flies at our open sores
>as if we were quartered melons in the market!
>as if this were not *our* ancestral pre-Columbian soil!
>as if the planets had not sung promises at *our* birth!
>Enough!
>Better to go down at once,
>head lifted, eyes burning, teeth asnarl,
>than slowly, with our tails between our legs!

And go down you will, under machine-gun fire . . .
but for one day at least
the two-legged
will not enjoy the luxury
of ignoring your mangy sides,
your inconvenient brown heaps of defiance.

Dogs of San Miguel—
you that are ghosts already,
you that look like ghosts,
you whose ghostly doom is on the humane society's timetable—
even I who care most
am forbidden to be haunted by you,
to groan at sight of your rotting ribs
outside the novelty window
where well-stuffed button-eyed pups
await the next tourbus explosion;
my concern must be for the one-eyed Indian woman
so disturbing to the charm of San Miguel,
withering in her dark shawl,
who may be next on the timetable.

I am forbidden, forbidden to be haunted by you;
get one of your own to howl.

IN THE GENEVE LOBBY: *Mexico City*

After six blocks of rain
over, under, around and through the bones of
these foolishly sandaled feet,
you clop-clop finally past the great front doors of the Geneve,
wait in line for the room key,
then start your long trek through the lobby
where dry guests wet their gullets: chatting, idly staring . . .
until you want to yell out: Hey!
Don't you see that I'm drenched to the skin,
that my socks hold a pailful of icy water each! . . .

And you feel that even if you came in with a head
half lopped off and bleeding,
they would still chat, sip, stare idly—
that even if you never made it back
through the great front doors
but melted into one of the beggar women
or cripples out among the puddles
the dry scene would go on . . .

And you realize that this is the way,
that to batter against the way would be childish, useless,
that these chatters, sippers in the lobby of the Geneve
are not among the worst but the best:
they do not kick or rob the beggar women
or curse the cripples silently
for spoiling the gay streetscapes of the Zona Rosa;
no—they are the very ones whose heartbeat
gives a beggar cause for hope day after day;
and, besides, that you're no better, if as good;
that, were you among the dry at the Geneve
and one came in with a drenched yell,
you too would idly stare . . .

And so, the length of the arrogant public lobby,
a loneliness develops inside you and envelops you long before you
          arrive at the elevator,

the stapled aluminum box
that will take you three floors closer
to the God they have agreed upon,
and it comes to you that out of such loneliness
they created him—
as if he, who flooded us in the first place,
would care beans about our drenched yell!

And why should a god,
chatting, sipping away in the long lobby of space,
stare any less idly
than they among whom you are walking,
you their own born brother?

TOLUCA: The Friday Market

How, since it is Friday,
can you not take the bus to Toluca?

Though the old paths from stand to stand
are paved,
still the flimsy bits of canvas tenting,
jeered at by wind and sun,
attempt to do their work with dignity
—unlike the Aztec, an infant humped on her back,
whining a willingness to hear your mean price
for her masterly baskets;
still a child, three huge disoriented chickens
slung upside-down over her head,
buckles and runs, runs and buckles,
reaches her family and collapses;
still the splendid and atrocious wares
forever waiting, waiting side by side:

the cactus leaves, cooked into goodness;
the deep-fried surreal stomach-walls of cows;
the dozen tacos, desperate for attention,
forced finally into a buyer's bag.

How, since it is Friday, your one and only Friday,
can you not take *something* from Toluca:
if only a machine-made leather belt (well haggled down)
and eleven slides
which may or may not develop three weeks hence
into the bright garb, the drained life
of the clusters you interrupted:
faces suddenly appalled,
afraid you have stolen their soul
and are carrying it home in your camera
without even bargaining for it;
not even leaving—
as would be proper for these ancient bartering grounds
haunted by so many ravished souls and prices—
yours in exchange.

NAFPLION: Snapshot

It is far from dark
but already the sun
has built his arc
over Nafplion.
We make our choice
of foods, pretending
no inner voice
declares: *It is ending*.

Four days welded together, a fifty-face centipede,
crawling out of and into museum, restaurant, bus,
crisscrossing the melon-ripe, spectacular Peloponnese,
we'd stood with Apollo's ghost, beheld Clytemnestra's blood,
bathed in the Gulf of Argos, over an aged bridge

entered Arcadia just as a shepherd was guiding his flock
toward the slope of Mt. Erymanthus, gazed into pans for our pick
of lamb-stew, moussaka, vine-leaves, okra, learned to lodge
at hotels named Oracle, Pericles, Halcyon (all night long
trucks rolled over our visions, toilets spasmodically flushed),
learned to emerge from a shower half-frozen, half-burned,
       half-washed,
after the seventh playing learned which tune would be sung
next on the guide's cassettes, learned gradually which name
goes with a face, which are in pairs, in threes, and who
comes from Toronto, from Budapest, Turin, who's probably gay,
who teaches music, psychology, who remains in her room.

       Tables propped
       together, they smile
       at my Kodak, grouped
       family style,
       having just skoaled
       with retsina wine
       a two-year-old
       granddaughter of mine.

Behind the fortress hill of Nafplion painfully sets
the sun: if the picture happens to turn out well, which is doubtful,
I promise solemnly, head by head, there'll be a hatful
printed and sent aloft to each of our argonauts.
—It is ending, no doubt of it, ending—more than this dinner party.
The talk grows closer than ever; tomorrow's a word that hurts,
but it will come; the bus will start, and perhaps, when it starts,
some will agree to meet on the Parthenon steps at nine-thirty
to drink the full of the moon; perhaps they really will meet;
but inwardly the scattering will have begun already:
after five days on the road we'll be feeling soiled and seedy,
we'll be seeking unruined showers; gradually, with regret,
as the bus nears Athens, we'll think of differences; the trip
will fall into focus; our minds will return to family faces,
flight confirmations, a tour of the islands (as good as this is,
we hope); for a while we may hunger to see one another take
       shape . . .

ATHENS: *Through Wide Open Shutters*

Through wide open shutters
for the last time on me
come the breeze from the Saronic Gulf or the mountains beyond
      Lykabettos,
the two same voices quarreling since dawn,
a hammering from a nearby workshop,
a vacuuming still nearer,
a shriek of wheels stopped short on Ermou Street, or Voulis.

This morning, on the broken toilet seat, studying down the airshaft
those slovenly kitchen noises which had wakened me,
I said to myself—
suddenly in love with the wretched seat and sounds—
tomorrow this will happen, but not to me.

All week, in fact, occasionally,
I have made silent, silly goodbyes
to the Parthenon, of course, but also
to the ancient streets, lovely once,
      ugly now, around the flea market,
to the tiny tenth-century church
      sitting on the sidewalk
      under the office building's arm
      like a shrivelled nanny with her fullgrown grandson,
to the marble Byron, eternally ebbing in the arms of Greece,
to the young at young Karaiskaki,
      65,000 raging for 40,000 seats,
      hearts high, fists high, voices at last high
      after seven years of beatings, steel bars, barbed wire,
      honoring Theodorakis, in whom each
      had been exiled, with whom each was now home,
      and his poets, Seferis, Neruda,
      whose funerals it had been dangerous to attend,
to the middle-aged at agéd Herod Atticus
      rapt, returning the love of Rostropovich's cello,
      rising at the close, rooted,
      as if to keep his last note frozen.

I have wanted to write in smoke on the blue above Athens: *Iasos*!
Iasos to each and all, before they turn ghost on my New York
        pillow
while I, but the latest of many ghosts,
am replaced on this pillow
by one who, eyes closed, in undershorts,
still unaware that the toilet seat is broken,
takes for the first time through wide open shutters
this quarreling, hammering, vacuuming,
this gulf or mountain breeze.

DELPHI: Slide 62

I know we're only one day into the tour;
I know it's nearly eight (you've checked your watch
three times); I know, no matter where we're at,
the slides come off, TV comes on at half
past eight. Last night you bristled at my hint
that all the slides of Greece were home, and all
in order, and we hadn't seen them yet.

Still, though you didn't ask, let me explain
this one your mother's after me to scrap.
You see my profile downcast toward those streaks?
You see the four girls grinning? We had just
caught up with them, and in the nick of time.
While seven gems of the museum posed
for me (the ones you saw just now in seven
seconds—seven!! for the Sphinx of Naxos,
the Charioteer, the War of Gods and Giants!!)
off to Castalia'd gone the bus—from there
whoever was missing could *walk* back to town!

[109]

What happened next was not your mother's fault.
She'd climbed her soles off on that holy slope
which was, to her, not holy. Had I said:
"You take the bus. I'd like to stay awhile"—
she'd not have balked; she knew what the book told:
how pilgrims cleansed themselves in it before
facing the word of Pythia, she who drank,
then prophesied. *One still can recreate*
that world of oracles by drinking from
the old Castalian spring, the landscape too,
and all the glories of the sacred grounds.

No need to wake her smile—or, worse, her yawn—
by adding what Castalia meant to *me*:
fount of the Muses, drink my veins have craved . . .
And she'd been quite a sport, hobbling all day
in step with kids a third our age. So, swinging
her hand, I said, "Let's catch the bus, okay?"
—We strode! Each sign along the road, however,
pointed Castaliaward, pulling my soul
that way. There sat the bus! time still to drink . . .

The girls—you see them grinning? They'd just watched
this weird expression cross my profile downcast
toward the dry well that Homer, Sappho drank from
in dreams, that Pythia in her exultations
drank from in fact, then uttered prophecy!
These streaks were all *I* found of it; the girls
pointed "up yonder" where they'd had a drink.
No time to seek it. The bus snarled. Time only
for one slide: the dry basin, my weird face,
and the girls grinning as I mumbled something
about how I'd been waiting all my life
to slake my thirst here.

Back at the Hotel
Oracle (next to the Pythia, by the way)
sipping my coke—a favorite drink in Delphi—
it struck me that I'd come five thousand miles
for nothing . . . *should* have said "I'll stay awhile . . ."
and sought the spring! Well—six weeks have gone by;
the hurt is down (though I may, after all,
remove Slide 62). And in one way
it's for the best. If inspiration fails me,
I can explain it as Castalia's failure.
How could one possibly excuse himself
if there *were* water, not just wretched streaks;
if one *had* placed his lips where Pythia
placed hers before her chantings rocked the world?

HERAKLEION: The Hidden Beach

There was this taxi driver
who fast-talked an "arrangement" from the airport;
the official who coolly beheld us
buckling under gray hair
and luggage and the lack of a room;
the hotel desk arrogant
in seven languages;
the vendor whose peaches doubled
when set on a tourist scale;
the Class A *mädchens* strawing
lemonade on the roof
who answered in ice-cubes: *Nein*,
I could *nicht* be their scrabble partner.

So we fled to the life-giving sea.
Safe in the lap of the fortress,
safe from the eyes at the roof-pool,
safe in the arms of the reefs,
forty-five bathers reveled—
splashing each other, gorged
on honey-soaked Saturday pastries
sold from a makeshift half-wagon:
one Stavros so fat, his suit
was a blown-up tube, one Kostas
so scrawny, his ribs were a sunlit
squadron, a girl unconcerned
that her playful right breast had almost
slid free of the bikini,
an infant shedding his fear
step by step, hand in father's.

As we peeled and slowly got into
the Creteness of our first peach
careful to drop not even
a bit of its skin on the rocks,
a soldier forgetting Cyprus
for one delirious moment
stealthily looked around,
peeled off all but his trunks,
rolled up his uniform, hid it
in a crevice, and—awkwardly plunging,
his humanhood slowly reviving—
sank himself in with the bathers.

To put it one way: you turned
a corner unmarked on the map,
and there in the sea, in the sun,
forty-five Saturday swimmers
suddenly came into being.
Or, to put it another way:

as we swam in our sea, sun, laughter,
there suddenly came into being
in business trousers and shirt
with his hat-and-handbag wife
one of that passing kind
in bus-windows, airports,
who ate, however, part
of a Cretan peach, instead
of our hearts, and trained on us
not a Kodak cannon
but the trembling lens of love.

CRETE: The Farewell

Not to the waiter, whose sleight-of-hand checks
needed checking, the airways cashier, metallic,
the hotel clerk, lord of his lobby, the policeman fit to be tied,
but to the father kissing his baby in the Sunday stroll
at Aghios Nikolaos, the bootmaker hammering
in his Rethymnon doorway, the caves of Matala
from which young underwear hangs drying,
the pitiful thrones of Knossos, Mt. Ida darkly mourning
over the bullfighter phantoms at Phaestos,
Herakleion's thick walls, which held out the Turks
for twenty-three years, which hold
the bones of Kazantzakis now, but not his spirit—
to these, since they neither heard us nor spoke to us,
the farewell can be, as the greeting was, silent but deep.

THESSALONIKI: Three Sleeps

1.

I don't blame you that my first night's sleep was fitful;
deep inside your womb you nestled me well
in a back room on the seventh floor—
not like those tour-towns swaggering till four A.M.
No, you are a town of workfolk,
take your sleep to heart,
get up at six.
But how, even in your stillness, could one stay asleep
surrounded by your swarms of lively ghosts:
those of your old town, high near the wall,
and of the older town, its agora half-showing;
Alexander himself on horseback ready to explode south;
Dimitrius, bleeding forever in the heavy embrace of your shrine;
the janissaries butchered all at once in your round tower;
Ataturk, new-sprung from his mother's womb and yours,
opening for the first time incendiary eyes;
Hitler's hostages—300 Greeks per German;
and all your Jews, sixty thousand,
saved from the Inquisition once, but now
proceeding with packages again, to a "better location";
Efstratia Nikolaidu, fifteen years old,
who would now be thirty-nine,
shot down in your prison-yard, fist high.

2.

In the afternoon of the second day,
filled with your ancient marble finds
and the feudal weavings of your artisans
and your waves, winds, sunrays washing through us
and your octopi dancing on the line, hung out to dry,
and your fresh-caught mackerel, tenderly fried to order,
home, exhausted and full, we came to our seventh-floor room
and lay down on your good large bed,

and as we worked at the crossword puzzle
something better crossed our minds.
Let the young in Crete, in Athens, packsacks on their backs,
think what they think of grayheads, whom they pass without a
         sign.
Afterward we slept beyond dreaming for two hours.

3.

The second night was different.
What woke me was, I guess, your deep-fried pastry
(corkubinia, they called it)
of which I'd had two wildsized helpings.
How, even in your stillness, could one stay asleep?
It is not every man who has a ticket
for the next bus to Byzantium.

MACEDONIA

1.

I bought a ticket to Byzantium;
I boarded a bus to Istanbul.
I bought a ticket to the Blue Mosque,
Topkapi, St. Sophia,
Leander and Hero ablaze in her tower,
the sinister windings of my dream-bazaar,
and all the goldsmiths hammering the Golden Horn of Yeats.
I boarded a bus in a real Thessaloniki thunderclap,
farewells really wept,
the electrical storm catching up at Kavala,
darkness choking us, rain stoning us, lightning and thunder
aimed at us like judgment from divine Mount Athos,

a judgment on me (hinted my wife)
for dragging her off to Byzantium (ha!)
though we'd probably be dead before the border.

As I slid still lower in my seat,
so as not to be noticed by an irritated god,
the driver, whose windshield wipers showed
two feet of wet death ahead,
started a cassette; at the first measure
a clapping began, a singing, a dancing of arms
aloft in the lightning,
and so till the tape ended.
Then quickly, outwitting grimness,
a voice began, insolently calm,
a raconteur risen from the storm, as Venus from the sea:
each tale applauded with lessening laughter
as the wind's noose tightened.
One more cassette:
the clapping defiant now, first seat to last,
as the bus groped forward, five miles an hour, toward Turkey,
toward a three-hour probing of luggage and passports,
toward Istanbul, from which hate had driven them,
toward the mother with risky blood-pressure,
the father whose business still broke even.
And now, since *such* could sway in time to melody and storm
as if the windshield wipers were metronomes,
suddenly the thunder was Persia's hooves
about to learn Samothrace;
the lightning was Turkey's blades, at last contrite
inside Topkapi Palace;
the rain was Hitler's bullets,
four wars back.
Greekly I thrust my arms aloft, and clapped, and sang.
Thus the night grew meek ahead of us.
Unscathed, we passed to Xanthe, slept like babes
in a Class D, backstreet hotel.

2.

Next day, exactly as my wife predicted,
our bags were lifted out
on both sides of the border,
sifted, shifted, strewn about
in orderly disorder,
every page of every passport scrutinized
backwards, forwards, every face inspected
as if cunningly disguised.

Then Istanbul: daylong, nightlong, tranced in the honk
of cabs, the insolence of clerks,
trouble,
roared bazaar-arrays of gem and junk,
Topkapi's welcomeway a growl of rubble,
the Golden Horn a fly-mad sump of rotted arks,
at the Blue Mosque
a crippled beggar picturesque
in his wheelbarrow, postcard-barkers thick as worms
at St. Sophia's corpse—and fears
of Hero's tower likewise ringed by souvenirs:
cheap poems
baked on tiles . . .
cheap styles
"hand-etched in Anatolia" . . .
—Byzantium, ha!

MADRID: Coming Home

Though I admire the turning of one's cheek,
Christ's is no easy life to imitate.
I did, I did
resent the fact that Franco's death was late
and gentle, that the tyrant lay in state,
that History did not wreak
vengeance before my coming home, Madrid.

When finally the plane fare had been paid,
blizzards and other business ringed me round.
The marvel slid
out of a brain that otherwise could pound
into submission the most pompous sound
December ever made:
"July will bring me home to you, Madrid!"

Each bough of April dipped with bugle-beaks;
"The time is near!" they probably declared.
But I, amid
their music, was more readily ensnared
by mutterings of mischief hatched or bared;
whole days went by, whole weeks
without the gasp: "I'm coming home, Madrid!"

Halfway through June, the sundeck's peeling red
entranced me, and the failing lawn. In dreams
I still bestrid
legions of dandelions, that mocked my schemes
and slaughters with their green, defiant screams.
Not once in my June bed
did I sit bolt upright and cry: "Madrid!"

Even as the airport's bulletin board
proclaimed that 904 would leave on time,
a bawling kid
caught at me, then the headline of a crime.
Dialing a sick aunt with my last dime,
I did not say one word
about my coming home to you, Madrid.

At dawn Iberia hove in view. I should
have risen with an inward shout, at least;
but we were bid
pull out our tables for a final feast;
poor sense, poor nerves, poor nescafé increased
the toilet lines; I stood
in place and heard: "One hour until Madrid."

Coruña passed; the cockpit spat a name:
below there . . . by that river . . . what? León?
Valladolid?
No matter—all at once we had been drawn
into the Guadarramas, flushed with dawn
peak after peak, and came
at last into the outskirts of Madrid.

All new . . . all prosperous . . . all rearranged . . .
Only the hills stayed firm. It made me feel
the way El Cid
might, if by miracle he found Castile
after nine hundred years: automobile
stampedes, where lambs had granged . . .
all changed . . . estranged . . . all but your name, Madrid.

Two hours I benched on your most populous street,
searching each passer's brow: perhaps in one
the stanzas hid
of what I hummed—your song, "No pasaran!"
Perhaps the book-clerk, when she saw me run
toward Lorca's shelf, would greet
my eyes with eyes of welcome to Madrid.

Of all who—with bare fist, back to the wall—
had stopped the tanks, was not one witness left?
Had Franco rid
your air of its best echoes, set adrift
your loveliest phantoms? Were you too bereft
of memory to recall
what lodestone drew me home at last, Madrid?

Nightfall. I lug to the eleventh floor
my bones and questions. In the looking-glass
under each lid
a bag sits brooding; sideburns (thick as grass
above stopped mouths that howled "They shall not pass!")
run gray. . . . Who was it swore,
the day you fell, he'd yet come home, Madrid?

[119]

SEVILLA: July 18th

We arrived
not on the birthday of Bizet or Byron,
but on July 18th, the anniversary
of Franco's fist.

      Awaiting the menu del dia,
      while sipping your charm, your sangria,
      we watched on TV, Sevilla,
      the matador's ritual call,
      the crowd's *Olé! olé*!
      devouring—one and all—
      at five in the dying day
      the ear of an outmatched bull.

Although suspicious, Carmen of the world,
I let you try seducing me:
    such plazas, barrios! your Santa Cruz!
    Giralda, long-necked flamenco dancer
    about to set her pious skirts awhirling at the first bell . . .
As a cocotte still in her prime leans under a street lamp,
you leaned your whitewashed face with dark wrought-iron balcony
        lashes,
waiting, if not for me, then for another,
success a million times proven.

Below your mantilla of towers, below the lashes and skirts,
I smelled you out
as Lear smelled out his daughters:
    But to the girdle do the gods inherit,
    beneath is all the fiends' . . .

      As we filled on your fruit, your tortilla
      and asked for the bill, Sevilla,
      the bullring of Madrid
      filled with a bullringful
      of your Guardia Incivil—
      eighteen thousand—enough
      to do as their grandfathers did,
      to play it equally rough
      in the name of Colón and El Cid—

to work their patriot will,
to show their matador skill,
come in for a scarlet spill
and fetch home as souvenirs,
at eighteen to one, the ears
of a thousand Lorcas—*olé*!
as eighteen marched him away . . .

You pretended not to know of it, Seville,
fanned yourself just a bit more swiftly;
—who, after all, expects a Carmen
to be mixed up with such things?

Now your official guidebook in four languages repeats
your every charm as Lorca sang it, now his poems
in sumptuous leather, like the prize ear of a bull,
keep the pesetas rhyming in your pocket,
while everywhere the posters, everywhere
graffiti of that special kind one comes to recognize,
honor his killers and their grandsons
who itch to leadpipe from their doors at night
the new "traidores y perjuros":
      VIVA FRANCO! VIVA POLICIA! ADELANTE LAS
            FUERZAS NACIONALES!
      ARRIBA ESPAÑA! ARRIBA EL 18 DE JULIO!
      ARRIBA DIGNITA, HUMANITA, PAZ ETERNA!

I look you over, smell you out a day or two,
hum you a new habanera:
    there's hell, there's darkness, there is the sulphurous pit,
    burning, scalding, stench, consumption; fie, fie, fie!

Cunning city, bent on winning me
one way or another!
On the last day I push through surrendering byways;
your Civil Guard salute me;
your grocers come out of their shops
to repeat with Franciscan patience
which are the turns to the Charity Hospital;

your nun there, proud
of every brushstroke by Murillo and Leal,
leaves us alone with her treasury of slides and books;
on the way back to the hotel, your families love-touch,
two grown girls, each with an arm inside grandfather's arm,
share with him, from your merchant's makeshift bag,
a 1/4 kilo of cashews.

—Giralda's bell strikes three . . . perhaps now she is whirling . . .
Is it that which wakes me, or the air conditioner,
or the vision that carries over from my sleep?
> Once again there rounds a corner,
> face full of peace and white beard,
> a slow Andalusian, savoring his path, a boy beside him . . .
Suddenly I know: this would be Lorca now,
if, as his friends begged, he had fled:
> just finishing a jug of sangria, pointing to a disciple
> the special charms of the Plaza de la Falange,
> which will soon have its old name again . . .

> > O city of souvenirs!
> > O city of bullring cheers!
> > Strike your castanets hard!
> > Keep, for the time I stay,
> > their slashing tread from my ears:
> > eighteen, still marching away
> > on the night of the grimmest day
> > of Granada's grimmest of years
> > her proud, imprudent bard
> > to make him decisively pay
> > for "The Song of the Civil Guard."

I will not return, Seville; you are bad for my blood pressure.
It is hard to love and hate at the same time—
enough that I have my own town to deal with:
the same dark rumblings, still hidden in its skull,
shrieked forth in black graffiti from your whitewashed walls.
If I stayed one more day and were true to my best self,
eighteen bullets would find me too.

CÓRDOBA: *Nocturne*

Now, in the dog-days of July
(the dog-nights too) there's not a breeze
for Córdoba to lullaby
her overnight dependents; these,
having no choice but to comply,
accept the brash disharmonies
of plodding bus and prodding car
and squalling square and braying bar
a mile from Mosque and Alcazar.

They sleep. But sometimes an unease
wakes them. They wonder: Where am I?
For which hotel have I the keys?
Is this Madrid's, Toledo's sky?
It comes to them: Maimonides,
Lucan and Seneca let fly
their lightnings here; and not so far
from where those lucent phantoms are,
Gabirol blazed; here set his star.

GRANADA: *The Rose*

You leveled with me, Granada;
you didn't once overcharge;
you walked out of your way to show me my way;
you really meant it when you said *De nada*!
—so I'll level with you.

Of course I loved your beauties—Lorca taught me how;
but neither Alhambra's picturesque wealth
nor Albaicin's picturesque poverty brought me,
neither the gypsies' hot freedom on their hill
nor the cold imprisonment of Fernando and Isabella.

I came, after forty years,
to find the center of Lorca's life
and leave a rose there.

At eleven this morning I shall board the bus for Málaga
having left no rose,
although I know where it should be placed.
Perhaps it was the fahrenheit that stopped me,
or my wife's plea that I do nothing "controversial."

But in fact at the end it grew clear
that Lorca needs no flower;
his name bursts richer than the gardens of the Generalife.
It was I who needed to bring it and find its proper place
—I, whose mouth opened because his was shut,
I, whose weakness feeds on his strength.

And you, Granada, you need it
—though I am a small poet, seldom anthologized,
and one rose more or less is perhaps not important
in a city of many roses.

When you have erased the name of Valdes
from that street behind the post office,
when you have finished with the statue of José Antonio,
when you have renamed the Square for him whose eyes caressed it
at all hours from the Acera del Casino window,
whose shoes increased its price each time he stepped across it—
then I will come again;
I have learned how to wait, but this time
it will not be for long.
I will come to you, Granada,
and place my rose at the feet of his statue,
for whatever one rose is worth.

MÁLAGA: A Prayer

Into a great firefly, without guile
alighting on this long gray stem of shore,
Málaga turns, mile upon brilliant mile,
suddenly, and for a little while
dances defiance of the sea's dark roar.

The lighthouse beams a vessel toward its dock:
this night no mariners are to be lost.
They disembark as mindless of the rock
as motorists are of the moon-round clock
that tries to warn what hour it's forty past.

Touched by such light, all shades of voices, faces
blend for one moment. Ah! the breeze!—whose promise
drew us together from those parched, far places . . .
Málaga, firefly, do not vanish from us!

ZUDIOSKA

Smug in her Adriatic noon, Dubrovnik beams.
Within her walls, unconquered and intact,
was much to save—with guns or cunning.
It is all on file in the Rector's Palace.

The streets, in conscious harmony,
flow down from her twin hills
to merge in the Placa, where tourists go
marveling, that after a thousand years
in this world of wounded columns, ravished mausoleums,
no stone is vexed.

Here stands Zudioska, street of the Spanish Jews.
(Dubrovnik took in their banished scrolls;
not often made them wear the yellow badge,
pay special fees, stand trial for ritual murder.)

Ask no question of the stones. Go past.
You will find nothing peculiar on Zudioska.
Women dry their wash.
Children throw their ball.
A cartload rumbles down the narrow steps.
No room is vacant.
There are customers enough in the cafe.

Across from the cafe a door is open.
At the first landing the rabbi awaits you.
On the second landing is the synagogue—
six hundred eighteen years old.
The worshippers await you, though one cannot see them.

Ask no question of the stones.
The Jews had names, but what's the difference?
had women, children, trades—but what's the difference?
It is all on file, no doubt, in the Rector's Palace.
The rabbi could tell you:

> two hundred Jews dwelled on this street.
> The Italians came, and put us on Rab.
> The Germans came, and took us to Auschwitz.
> Seventeen crawled home, and not one child.

> We sweep the floor of the synagogue each day.
> We hold our service without a *minyan*.
> Soon the synagogue will be perfectly silent,
> as silent as the perfect stones of the city,
> a museum with a guard collecting fees.

> God saved us from the quake of 1667.
> Nobody saved us in 1943.
> And you, if you were Dubrovnik, would you have cried
> > *Shame*!
> as they checked off each name and shoved us into the boat?

Zudioska drowns in shadow.
The Placa runs in light.
Shield your eyes when you come back into the light
or the beaming stones will burn them as if you are crying.